DANCING WITH NUMBERS

DANCING WITH NUMBERS

GROW A FINANCIALLY HEALTHY BUSINESS AND CHOREOGRAPH THE LIFE YOU WANT

TRICIA M. TAITT

NEW DEGREE PRESS

COPYRIGHT © 2022 TRICIA M. TAITT

All rights reserved.

Author photo credit: Raj Bandyopadhyay

DANCING WITH NUMBERS

*Grow a Financially Healthy Business and Choreograph
the Life You Want*

ISBN   979-8-88504-997-9   *Paperback*
          979-8-88504-998-6   *Kindle Ebook*
          979-8-88504-999-3   *Ebook*

Table of Contents

SECTION 1

STRETCH

Introduction

Do you ever feel messy, disorganized, insecure, or completely out of your league when it comes to managing your finances?

Are you good at math and spreadsheets, but analyzing financial reports puts you in fog?

Does your bookkeeper do a good job tracking and reviewing your numbers, but you want some deeper insights and advice?

Well, you are not alone! I'm here for you.

If you have been in business two, five, even ten years or more, your company is growing, but you aren't getting the answers you need to questions about your financials, you probably need the analytical and strategic mind of a chief financial officer (CFO). Unlike trying to figure things out on your own, with a general business adviser, or in a mastermind group, working with a CFO will reveal the story behind your numbers. Those insights will help you make critical business decisions and build a financially fit company that pays you what you need to live the life you want. Getting clients to these results is the goal of my company, FinCore (https://fincorestrong.com), and a big driver behind writing this book.

THE MUSE BEHIND THIS BOOK

When people ask, "What inspired you to write this book?" I reflect on the hundreds of questions, emails, and direct messages I fielded from small business owners who desperately needed capital, counsel, action steps, and information to keep their businesses afloat in 2020. Many did not know their numbers, have emergency funds, nor have the documents or financial track record to access capital. The 2020 pandemic and global recession revealed how many financial issues plague small business owners, especially women and women of color (WOC) entrepreneurs. It exacerbated the fact that if you do not have a finger on the pulse of your financials, your business is at great risk of failure. At one point during the COVID-19 pandemic, I read that 41 percent of Black-owned US businesses closed from February to April 2020, the largest closure rate of any racial group. Latinx business owner activity fell by 32 percent, and Asian business owner activity dropped by 26 percent (Robert Fairlie, 2020).

The intention of this book is not to shine a light on the racial wealth gap and gender inequalities that play out in the economic aspects of our lives, nor to comment on why women-owned businesses receive less venture capital funding than their male counterparts. The goal of this book is to focus on what we can do to control the narrative and improve the chances of our businesses growing healthily in terms of cash flow, profits, and impact. I believe the primary way to do that is through financial education: leveling up your knowledge and getting comfortable with your numbers.

This book is for women entrepreneurs, it's for women of color (WOC) entrepreneurs, it's for creative entrepreneurs, it's for the non-numbers people. It's for those who were once fearful of numbers, are brave enough to admit they need help, and are now ready to take them on. I wrote this book to play my part in your financial empowerment and let you know you have a champion in your corner.

The image under the chapter titles is a version of the Adinkra symbol for wealth, abundance, and prosperity. Adinkra symbols were originally created for textiles worn and used by the royalty of ancient Ghana and Côte d'Ivoire. I placed the image at the start of each chapter to serve as a reminder of what is possible for you and your business when you're *Dancing with Numbers*—wealth, abundance, prosperity (Afrolegends.com blog, 2014).

Three other situations inspired the words on these pages.

Inspiration #1: the consultation
Inspiration #2: the woman with the credit card
Inspiration #3: the rehearsal process

#1: THE CONSULTATION

For over fifteen years, Ameera has led an architectural design and construction company, started by her father. She grew up in the business, so she knew the ins and outs of the work, their clients, and even the names of their employees' children. She was well equipped to take over when her dad retired, but she never got a firm hold of the financial side of the business. Even though she had a business manager doing the bookkeeping, she never quite understood the business's performance and felt pretty embarrassed about it. By the time we met, she was ready to get help fixing this situation.

She said, "I want someone to help me strategize, make good decisions for the future, and hold my hand along the way; to review the numbers regularly, give insights, tell me where the problems are, and help me fix them; and to oversee the financial operations and speak on our behalf to our CPA and lenders."

I told her this is part of what we do at FinCore. Clients come to us looking for a financial partner whose super-power is numbers, so they can focus on harnessing the strengths of their own superpowers. Our promise is to *educate* small business owners around their financials, so they gain confidence in their own decision-making, *engage* in a healthier relationship with their numbers, and *elevate* their impact in their business, their communities, and their personal lives.

After my conversation with Ameera and many other experienced small business CEOs like her, I wondered, *How many owners need some good financial advice on demand, in one place where they can access it over and over again?*

That leads me to the woman with the credit card.

#2: THE WOMAN WITH THE CREDIT CARD

In 2008, I taught a financial literacy series on behalf of Citigroup and Operation Hope. A fifty-plus-year-old woman asked about building and maintaining good credit. She said her husband always managed all the finances, but now, without him, she wanted to build her own credit and get a credit card for the business.

I was surprised that a woman about the same age as my mother did not know this information, but I was so proud of her for taking advantage of that workshop to independently build her financial life. That moment made me realize how fortunate I was to grow up with savvy women who started teaching me about financial planning, investing, home ownership, and credit management from an early age. My dad and godfather were both CPAs who worked in the accounting and financial fields. But my earliest financial lessons came through observing the women.

My grandmother was one of the first "bookkeepers" I knew, keeping a ledger of how the household spent money in her native Trinidad and Tobago and as she built her personal wealth in the US. My aunts taught me about the importance of home ownership and investment. My mother taught me to budget and manage spending with a checkbook before I went off to Phillips Academy for high school at fourteen. She co-signed my first credit card when I was sixteen so I could build credit. People thought she was crazy to do it, but she trusted me. I guess you have to know your children. At twenty-two, I started my first job and contributed the maximum to my 401(k) plan every year. I probably lived off 60 percent of my gross salary.

I never forgot that woman in the financial literacy workshop. She made me realize everyone doesn't learn good financial habits and behaviors in childhood and unfortunately, they bring those limitations to their business life as adults. She inspired my life purpose and is another guiding light for this book.

#3: THE REHEARSAL PROCESS

During my finance career, I danced professionally; my first opportunity came through Dr. Charles Davis, affectionately called Baba Chuck Davis, by the dance community. Then in 2007, I joined the New York-based Forces of Nature Dance Theater, and in 2013, I joined the cast of the Tony award-winning Broadway musical, *Fela!* The level of passion, precision, and power it takes to perform on stage starts in the rehearsal process. Many dancers like myself start out overwhelmed by new choreography, uncomfortable with the movements, and insecure about how we will look on stage. Over time, we build our emotional, mental, and physical core until we are confident in our abilities to deliver a strong performance.

As a professional dancer and a CFO, I see many similarities between the journey dancers take to prepare for a big performance and the transition a business owner makes from taking a passive to an active role in their business's financial management. So, I've interwoven dance metaphors and imagery throughout the book.

In the same way that dancers must strengthen their physical core to be at peak performance, business owners must strengthen their financial core to grow to peak performance.

Such metaphors are also used to make the subject of finance more fun, engaging, and relatable instead of stress- and anxiety-provoking. I want all readers and listeners, especially my fellow women entrepreneurs, to dance with their numbers in a smooth salsa instead of a torrid tango, so they can grow by leaps and bounds and choreograph the lives they want. And in this book, you'll find the steps to do just that.

Step 1: Accept the invitation to dance, every day
Step 2: Uncover and remix old money scripts
Step 3: Smoove through the triggers
Step 4: Strengthen your core
Step 5: Get a financial choreographer and dance partners
Step 6: Grow to peak performance

PREPPING THE STAGE

You don't need an MBA or secret decoder to translate the book's concepts and lessons. It's laid out in a storytelling format so you can easily digest it. It includes strategies for financial management, practical applications of technical concepts, and stories of how business owners survived financial landmines, grew profitable businesses, and now walk confidently in their CEO shoes. The book can be read sequentially, or you can jump to the subject matter that speaks directly to the financial question or challenge you're facing now. Consider it your guide to becoming the chief financial officer of your business and your life.

We all know the story of Dorothy in the *Wizard of Oz* and *The Wiz*, a Tony award-winning Broadway musical that remixed the film. What I loved about this story is that Dorothy thought she needed the wizard's power to make her dream of going back home come true. But along the way, she found it took heart, courage, a brain, and most importantly, belief/faith to realize her dream (and a few savvy guides along the way to keep pointing her in the right direction).

Similarly, it takes heart, courage, smarts, and faith to be a business owner and journey down the winding, yellow brick road of entrepreneurship. For sure, many of the challenges you have faced on the yellow brick road were financial ones. How did you make decisions in the face of these difficulties? Did you call your CPA, your CFO, a mentor, a fellow business owner, your mastermind members? Or did you Google it and sit alone trying to figure it out by yourself?

Well, now you have this book and me, to guide you. I am your financial choreographer who shares strategies, lessons, and resources—on demand—whenever you need that help.

A GUIDE TO DANCING WITH YOUR NUMBERS

Within these pages, I share over twenty years of expertise garnered from my own experiences at the Wharton School of Business (University of Pennsylvania), Fuqua School of

Business (Duke University), Wall Street, and many years working in the trenches with business owners to help them level up their financial knowledge so they can grow forward.

Under Deepa Iyer's social change ecosystem, I identify as a *builder*, helping small business owners strengthen what's often the weakest part of their business, the finances. While I have nuggets in my book for business owners at every stage—existence, survival, success, growth, maturity—the lessons and advice are geared toward owners of small businesses who:

§ operate as the company's president or CEO full-time for at least three years;
§ have grown revenue to six or seven figures;
§ are ready to take control of their numbers; and
§ are humble or brave enough to ask for help.

The book includes:

§ actionable measures to advance your financial knowledge so you can better understand your business's performance;
§ tried and tested strategies to overcome financial obstacles; and
§ inspired stories from fellow business owners who have transformed from self-proclaimed "non-numbers people" to CEOs who now dance with their numbers.

Accept the Invitation to Dance, Every Day

You are the chief financial officer of your business and your personal life.

Let that sink in.

As small business owners, we wear so many different hats. One of the most important is that of a CFO, which means you have a fiduciary responsibility to make sure you are earning enough to live comfortably *and* keep your business financially fit.

Even if you hire an outsourced CFO to handle 80 percent of your company's financial matters, you should always keep your eye on the numbers at least 20 percent of the time, as the owner and chief decision maker. Now, you're probably thinking, *I started a business because...*

...I'm passionate about what I do.

...I wanted a more flexible work schedule.

...I grew dissatisfied with corporate America and wanted to be my own boss.

Or you're thinking, *I didn't start a business expecting to also play the role of a salesperson, HR manager, CFO, or any other position I'm not good at.*

The truth is, if you've been an entrepreneur long enough, you know the real deal. You must pay attention and stay connected to the numbers to maintain a financially healthy business. If the reality that "you are the CFO of your business and your life" finally sunk in today and stressed you out, don't fret!

ACCEPT THE INVITATION

Entrepreneurship extends its hand, inviting small business owners the opportunity to dance with their numbers, and it provides the stage for us to grow and stretch in ways we could not have imagined especially, around the parts of our business we don't love.

Do you accept the invitation? This is the first step toward dancing with numbers.

I often joke and compare being an entrepreneur to jumping off a cliff into the great unknown, every day. Even if your business grows to a decent revenue size, there will always be issues. New levels bring new obstacles. Accepting the invitation that entrepreneurship presents means also accepting the discomfort that comes with it. It means embracing the fact that while dancing with your numbers and working toward a better understanding of them, you will feel awkward, stumble, or fall flat on your face. But like any other pro, you get right up and keep going.

If you feel discomfort and fear about managing your finances because you don't have a business school degree or financial work experience, use that feeling to motivate you to either find the answers or the experts who can help you. The alternative is that fear will keep you frozen and the business stagnant.

GET PHYSICAL

To get comfortable with the uncomfortable Jayson DeMers, CEO of Email Analytics, suggests small business owners find short-term coping strategies, including breathing exercises, stretching, positive visualization, or brief periods of meditation (DeMers, 2020). Can you tell my coping mechanism is dance? When I rehearse with my dance company or party to soca music, I completely release the concerns and fears of being an entrepreneur and find renewed energy.

Fear is experienced in our minds, but it triggers a strong physical reaction. The brain alerts the nervous system, which sets a fear response into motion. Many of us experience an increase in blood pressure and heart rate, we breathe faster, and a fight-or-flight response may take hold. Since fear is experienced physically, I recommend engaging in a physical activity to counter it and channel that energy into something useful and productive—like our businesses (Healthbeat, 2020).

When you are calmer, you can focus on what needs to be handled. As an entrepreneur, that usually means making smart decisions based on real information, to keep income flowing and profitability in your sights. And that means knowing how to get and interpret the right financial information.

LEAN ON A PARTNER

Joshua had been manufacturing high-end, environmentally safe, handwoven silk and wool rugs for over fifteen years. He is a creative, a collector of ethnic artifacts, and a motorcycle aficionado.

Joshua looked at his bank account daily to determine the business's cash status. Since the rugs were manufactured internationally, he was always concerned about having enough cash to support the business between shipments. Clients paid 50 percent deposits upfront and paid the balance upon receipt of the rug. In the past, his financial person created complicated spreadsheets that he did not understand and therefore, completely dismissed.

As a creative person, Joshua needed to see information in an unconventional (yet structured) way to digest it. I created a cash flow dashboard with simple charts, so he knew what was coming in and what was expected to flow out of the bank account every week. At first, he looked at it and threw it aside, probably scarred from past "spreadsheet trauma." He had little connection to his numbers. His wife handled that side of the business, so he was free to create and make beautiful things. But he wanted more insights from his numbers, so I walked him through the dashboard every week until he became accustomed to it.

I analyzed three years of revenue and expenses and found a decline in revenue over a six-month period. I dug deeper into the three-year history of sales by customer and found that one of Joshua's best clients had not placed an order in about a year. He then pointed it out to his sales team, they contacted the client, and they immediately booked an in-person meeting with the client. As a result of the visibility into his financials and his team's efforts, the client placed a big order. Joshua finally saw the value in reviewing financials on a regular basis.

From that moment on, he requested the cash flow dashboard weekly and the other financial reports monthly. He relied on them to direct his priorities for the month. Joshua became open to learning more about his numbers and we scheduled monthly financial reviews. Joshua is just one of many "non-numbers" people who converted to someone who now dances with them.

JUST KEEP SWIMMING

Even though I have an MBA and formal business experience, I have realized my own discomfort. Sales and marketing did not feel natural to me in the beginning. I didn't want to sound "salesy," and I did not feel comfortable making the pitch nor asking for the sale. It felt desperate. But I knew that if I didn't convert leads into clients and turn clients into raving fans, there will be no cash and no business.

Coming up with marketing language for social posts and newsletters posed its own uphill battle. I tried to balance between sounding "authentic," toning down the technical jargon, and maintaining English writing etiquette. But nobody cared, liked, commented, or converted into clients. However, I kept at it. In the words of Dory, the royal blue tang fish in the animated film *Finding Nemo*, "Just keep swimming, just keep swimming."

With that in mind, I kept trying to figure out the sales and marketing approaches that felt right to me. It took years of trial and error, numerous lectures on sales conversion, and expert guidance to understand that the key to successful sales and marketing is storytelling and telling the customer exactly how you will relieve their pain or solve their problem.

One secret is to tell the customer exactly what they want to hear about how you can help, using their own words. Once they become clients, provide them with what they need to be successful. Operating in this way may feel like you're being patronizing or out of integrity. But customers want to know whomever they buy from or work with can solve the problem they specifically want help with and if your product or service can't do that, then tell them. It's okay to say, "This product/service is not the right fit for you at this time; I suggest this or that alternative."

Entrepreneurship gave me the platform to not only strengthen my sales chops but also to figure out what I'm great at and what I'm not so good at so I can better allocate my time and dollars.

SURROUND YOURSELF WITH THOSE WHO HAVE "BEEN THERE AND DONE THAT"

Luam K. is a dancer, celebrity choreographer, creative director, and senior television producer who was raised with little awareness about money management. She grew up in an era when parents didn't share much financial information with their children. Luam's parents wanted her to focus on her education and getting good grades. She learned that hard work eventually pays off with a good job and a good salary. But when she got to corporate America, the concept of earning a finite salary, regardless of the effort exerted, was illogical to her. So Luam pursued an entrepreneurial path as a teacher, choreographer, and later a creative director, to control her financial destiny.

The business of being an artist is a complex and unpredictable one. In the beginning, you must do a lot with a little and the money has to last until the next gig. Luam's first piece of advice to creatives would be to learn how to make a consistent, continuous stream of money that serves as the base income supporting your artistry. Then you would have the flexibility to pursue special projects and opportunities with bigger checks. Once you are no longer living check to check, the next step is to invest (in mutual funds, real estate, a managed portfolio, or other investments) and take risks that have the chance of a big return. When you have the money, do the most with it. Put your proverbial eggs in multiple financial baskets. Life events—children, marriage, taking care of parents, losing a big client or a home—can come from nowhere and hit you hard.

Step three is to figure out what trigger is going to accelerate your company's growth to the next level so it doesn't stay in slow and steady mode. Consider what kind of jobs you're getting, how you're positioning your brand, how you're utilizing your network to get into a higher paying position and who is at the top of the field you want to be in. Finally, have faith. Stay flexible and fluid, because according to Luam, "Sometimes God will just 'karate chop' your life and flip you into another direction, which happens to be the best direction for you."

Given all the lessons Luam has learned as a career creative, she created a financial literacy, dance, and business development program that teaches financial literacy to newcomers to the performance industry. She encourages her students and artist entrepreneurs to "be open to learning because as your business and personal brand grows there is more to know. Things change. What would have been a good investment or source of income a few years ago, may not be the best source for your business at a new stage. Do your research and have people in your corner who've been through the exact same thing you're going through, so you have the right information to make informed decisions."

CHANNEL FEAR INTO SOMETHING USEFUL

In an April 2018 *Harvard Business Review* article, professors James Hayton and Gabriella Cacciotti offered additional strategies for turning fear and discomfort of managing the numbers into something useful.

§ Practicing emotional self-awareness: Become aware of emotional changes, anticipate their impact on our thoughts, and use the awareness to limit the effects on decisions and actions.
§ Problem-solving: Use the feeling of fear as a signal to get busy problem-solving instead of stewing in the emotion. Take a deliberate, action-oriented approach. The action doesn't have to be a perfect one. Practice progress over perfection.
§ Learning is a powerful antidote, helping to mitigate one's doubts by increasing one's capabilities. James and Gabriella found that entrepreneurs overcome fear and discomfort through formal education and training as well as through information seeking by doing research.
§ Mentors and social support networks are a vital source of reassurance and constructive criticism along the process of overcoming fear and discomfort. Hearing from those who have "been there, done that" shifts negative thoughts and feelings.

Entrepreneurship gives small business owners many opportunities to dance with numbers and gain a healthier, more confident relationship with them if we give ourselves permission to make mistakes, feel awkward, and be vulnerable. Accept the invitation daily, keep learning, and seek expert and social support. Throughout the rest of this book, you will meet other entrepreneurs who have transformed their relationship to their numbers and found the FUN in FINANCE.

CHAPTER 2

Uncover and Remix Old Money Scripts

Stacy T. owns a scented candle-making company that sells to hospital gift shops and funeral parlors as well as direct to consumer. She grew up in a comfortable home with parents who had the means to cover the cost of running a household of five. Stacy's mother taught her how to make a little money stretch. As an adult, Stacey took pride in the fact that she was able to negotiate and do what her mother did. It felt like a game she was always good at, but she grew tired of living paycheck to paycheck. Stacey has worked hard for years but did not make enough from her business to take a proper vacation nor save for retirement. She does not have a second-in-command she trusts to take over the business in her absence.

Furthermore, Stacy struggles with invoicing clients and asking for payment. She said, "I know I'm worthy of the money, but I don't want to bother my clients. I create all of these stories about what they can and cannot afford and it stops me from invoicing the client and charging what I know I deserve." When I asked how she was paying the bills if she wasn't collecting from clients, she admitted to doing what she has always done: make a little money stretch. Her old money mindset was at play, preventing Stacy from getting paid, ultimately keeping income limited and the business stagnant.

The stage fright, resistance, or disregard you experience when looking at your bank account, reading financial statements, sending an invoice, asking for payment or a loan aren't just functions of being an entrepreneur. Your feelings, habits, and relationship with money were formed in childhood. They crystalized as you became an adult, and now that you are playing a lead role on the entrepreneurial stage, those feelings and habits have amplified. The spotlight is on you to make all the financial decisions. If you want to have a better relationship with the financial aspects of your business and your life, uncover and reframe the money mindset and behaviors that no longer serve you. This is the second step toward engaging in a harmonious relationship with your numbers.

FLIPPING THE SCRIPT

To help Stacy change her perspective and still have grace with herself, I suggested she think about her candle-making work—giving comfort to consumers in moments of grief—as an act of service. I asked her to consider that she is creating an experience with her candles for people to ease their burdens and that they would gladly pay for a chance to feel one moment of joy, relief, or ease with her scented candles. The customer probably wants to show appreciation by buying more candles and signing up for her subscription box. If Stacy doesn't invoice or charge consumers what she deserves, they don't get the opportunity to reciprocate.

The other thing I suggested she do is determine how much in salary she needs from her business to afford a vacation and start a SEP IRA. Whatever the dollar amount, she was to write it in bold numbers and pin it with a picture of the vacation spot somewhere near her work desk as a visible reminder of what she is working for. The last suggestion was to let Stacy's bookkeeper take the lead in collecting payment. That way, the bookkeeper plays the bad cop, standing on the front lines interfacing with the customer while Stacy remains a neutral party as a solution provider and problem solver. The worst-case scenario is a client is egregiously late with payment and Stacy's business attorney has to send them a demand letter.

Back in 2007, when I started teaching small business financial management workshops, I wondered why it was difficult for some to grasp the concepts. I tried to break down the technical speak into easily digestible bites. I knew the small business owners understood the importance of budgeting, paying debts on time, and actively managing cash flow, but they just couldn't seem to maintain healthy money management behaviors. Class participants often said they've taken many financial workshops, "but things don't stick."

Clients, embarrassed by their lack of knowledge and messy financial situations, would try to reassure me that they weren't completely unaware of their finances. They would say, "I'm pretty good at math." "After X years in business, I can pretty instinctively tell how to price a product." "We have our books in order." Sometimes this was true, but most times it was not. This also left me wondering what is underlying the emotion, the inability to change and adopt new, better money habits.

In search of answers, I spoke with Carolyn, a former investment banker and venture capitalist-turned-resident financial expert at SCORE, a partner of the Small Business Administration (SBA) that provides free mentorship to small business owners. I asked her why she thought owners were generally fearful around numbers, and she said, "I think it reminds them of eighth grade math class, when you know you have a quiz that you're going to fail. They are ultimately afraid to look stupid especially when it comes to their business, so they think, *I'm not good at math, so I will avoid dealing with it.*"

The other reasons she believes business owners are fearful of their numbers is that financial statements, bank statements, point of sales system reports, and other financial records are like report cards; business owners are almost afraid to look at their report card for fear it would tell them they're failing. When owners look at their numbers, it's often under unpleasant circumstances, such as at tax time when their CPA prepares the tax returns or when conversing with a lender or financial adviser who speaks in jargon. This makes the experience with numbers even more scary.

Carolyn said, "Who wants to feel like a failure or stupid when they have committed so much time, effort, and money to a venture?"

WOMEN BUSINESS OWNERS PERFORM

I wondered if Carolyn's rationale could also explain why less than 2 percent of women business owners in the US generated one million dollars or more in revenue in 2018 (Ventureneer, 2018); it's probably not that different today. We can't discount the years of social and economic injustices toward women that contributed to this ridiculous statistic. In 1988, the Women Business Ownership Act was passed, giving women business owners the right to apply for a loan without a male co-signer. That was not too long ago!

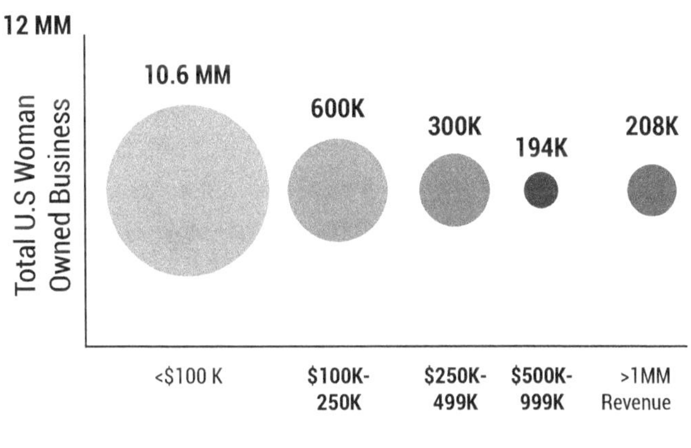

Research shows that many women-owned businesses show "constrained performance" (not to be confused with under-performance) due to factors like type of business chosen, access to capital, limitations on time to devote to a business due to family caregiving responsibilities, and fewer assets to invest (Marlow, S. and McAdam, M., 2013). But the US Department of Commerce's October 2010 report "Women-Owned Businesses in the 21st Century" suggests that women business owners have some part to play in stagnant revenue growth. "Female business owners, and women in general, are more risk- averse than men, especially when taking on financial risk. Such financial risk aversion could influence the type of business chosen, the amount and type of start-up and growth capital, and the desire to expand."

I believe the reason women entrepreneurs experience "constrained performance" is that they get caught in a never-ending cycle. Without the right financial preparation, training, and support they experience stagnant revenue and profit growth. FinCore's mission is to move 10 percent of these women from six figures of revenue to seven figures by helping them gain access to capital. Data shows that women entrepreneurs' revenue and employment growth accelerate once they hit the one-million-dollar revenue milestone—ultimately positively impacting the US economy.

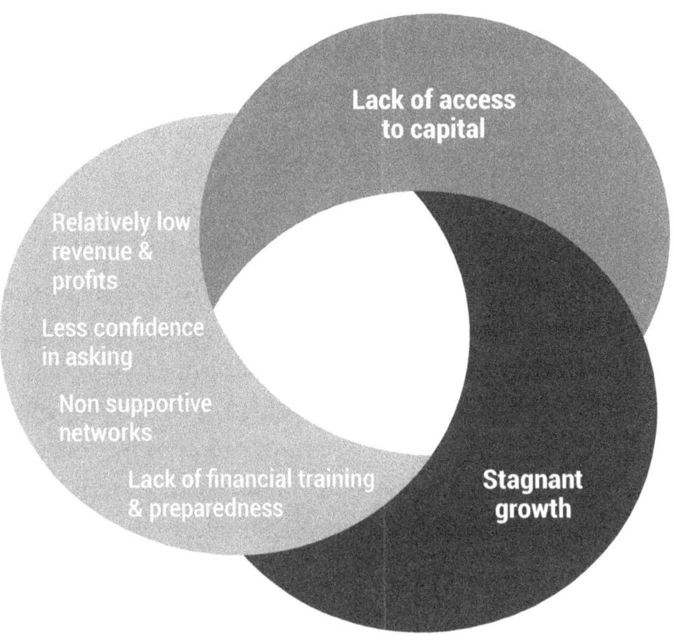

Citation: State of Female Entrepreneurship
She's Next: Empowered by Visa Report, 2019

To better understand the source of the "constrained performance," I asked about fifty business owners, women and men alike, about their earliest memories and lessons around money to see if there were differences in gender conditioning about money. Although it's hard to draw a definitive conclusion from a relatively small population, the people I interviewed surprisingly did not show a significant disparity in how the genders experienced money in childhood. Additionally, the financial challenges they experienced as business owners were the same as what they saw their parents and guardians struggle with. This insight helped me be a more compassionate and understanding CFO. When clients hire the CFOs at FinCore, they don't just get a professional who takes on the company's financial management responsibilities; they also get someone who guides and mentors them to be better financial stewards of their own businesses.

FINANCIAL THERAPY TO SHIFT THE MONEY SCRIPT

To assist clients ready to shift old disruptive money beliefs formed in childhood, I looked into a practice called financial therapy. The Financial Therapy Association (FTA) defines financial therapy as "a process informed by both therapeutic and financial competencies that helps people think, feel, and behave differently with money, to improve overall well-being through evidence-based practices and interventions."

The FTA, founded in 2008, is a non-profit organization conceptualized by researchers and practitioners who were interested in adapting treatment tools and techniques from marriage, family therapy, and psychology to the practice of financial planning and counseling. It was established so the practitioners could share information about their techniques with fellow counselors and researchers to validate the efficacy of their treatments.

Rick Kahler, a founding board member of the FTA, came into financial therapy after a divorce. Through that experience, he applied different modalities he learned to unearth and resolve his underlying issues with money. When I interviewed him, he recalled that in the beginning of FTA's existence, he and the other founders wanted to create a certification for financial therapists. A financial therapist needed to hold either an undergraduate degree in financial planning or an equivalent certification like the certified financial planner (CFP) certification. Or, they could hold a master's degree in the mental health field and then have a lot of experience in the other area. Rick was one of the FTA's first certified financial therapists.

Rick continued his studies, becoming a certified Internal Family Systems (IFS) practitioner. IFS is an evidence-based therapeutic modality. Rick now combines financial therapy with this modality, allowing him to dive deeper into why people get stuck around money. He, like other financial therapists, believes that every financial decision we make as adults is influenced by unconscious beliefs formed in childhood. These beliefs are called *money scripts.* While Kahler says the average person has fifty to two hundred unconscious money scripts, they generally fall into four money script categories: *money avoidance, money worship, money status, and money vigilance.*

§ Money avoiders associate money with greed and corruption and being a bad person. They also don't believe they deserve to have money.
§ Money worshippers believe money is the source of all freedom and joy and a better life, so they are always working to get more.
§ Money status people often grow up in low-income environments. They believe having more money and being in a higher socioeconomic class would increase self-worth.
§ Money vigilance is being generally cautious with money and tending to have good financial health. But these people struggle with spending money even for necessities and relaxing, and tend to be overly anxious about money.

I'm a money vigilant. Since my family ingrained in me sound money management practices around saving, investing, credit building, and long-term planning, I have pretty good money habits. However, it's difficult to take big investment risks because everything they taught was intended to keep me and my money safe. So I don't buy into market dips, day trade, or chase the latest investment opportunity. Entrepreneurship is the biggest gamble I've ever taken. I much prefer investing in real estate and businesses with steady cash flow because they feel safe. My current money habits were directly influenced by what I learned growing up. It has protected me, but it has also prevented me from enjoying certain rewards.

Be aware of how the money stories formed in childhood affect how you manage money today, as a business owner. Remember, you are not only the chief financial officer of your business, but you are also the CFO of your personal finances. If old money scripts are causing destructive and limiting money beliefs and stunting your ability to make good financial decisions for your business, and you can't change your behaviors cognitively, look to financial therapy to change those unhealthy behaviors around money.

THE STUCK PLACE

"Every financial behavior makes perfect sense, no matter how illogical it is to ourselves or other people, once we understand the underlying money scripts," Rick claims. "In every case when we get to that underlying belief, and it's causation, it makes perfect sense." Rick starts his therapy sessions by interviewing and evaluating patient's money habits until he finds a place where clients get stuck (e.g., opening credit card statements, doing the bookkeeping, filing taxes, saving money, being responsible with credit). He calls these trail-heads. He leads patients down a metaphorical trail to identify the source of what is blocking them and keeping them stuck.

Where people often get stuck is when a belief they have about money, usually formed during childhood, isn't work-ing anymore. It used to work but now the play has changed the circumstances. While the lines in Shakespeare's *Romeo and Juliet* work perfectly in that play, they become a disas-ter when recited in August Wilson's play, *Fences*. When this happens in your financial circumstances, it can cause your finances to go down the tubes. So Rick's second step during financial therapy sessions is to help the client connect the dots between their unhealthy behaviors around money and the money script they formed in childhood from a financial trauma. Here is an example of how that showed up with one of Rick's clients, Barbara.

Barbara, a very accomplished businesswoman, was having problems saving money. She made a nice salary from her business and had a nice home, but spent every dollar instead of stashing money away for retirement, building an emer-gency fund, or reinvesting in the growth of her business. She wondered why it was so difficult to save despite several attempts to do so, even while working with a financial adviser.

Rick helped her trace this behavior back to childhood when her parents took the money that she'd saved in a piggy bank, to cover emergency family financial situations. Rick asserts that children take in signals from the world around them regarding how money works and what they should or should not do with money. They translate what they see and hear into unconscious rules about life and money, which they hold as truth. When Barbara's parents took her money in the piggy bank, it probably started a series of messages and beliefs that she held as truths. They were reinforced a few more times through adolescence when money disappeared from her bank account and was used by her parents to support her family. Thus, the following money script was formed: "If I save money, it *will* disappear and not be there for me." She learned that to enjoy the benefit of money earned, it had to be spent immediately; otherwise, it would disappear. That's why she had trouble saving. Over a series of sessions, Rick helped her identify and then modify this money script to "If I save money, while it *could* disappear, it *could* also be there to support me in an emergency or retirement."

Unconscious money scripts that go unresolved can sabotage our future financial success. At least Barbara recognized she needed to make a change and sought help. She was also open enough to discover the source of her unhealthy behavior with money and worked toward shifting it. According to Rick, it is rare that money scripts are modified and behaviors changed simply because of cognitive recognition (awareness of the problem). Sometimes there needs to be an intervention (a trigger), an event, or experience that challenges our distorted thinking and causes so much pressure and discomfort that the only way to alleviate it is to make a change and face the fear that can come with change.

TRANSFORM YOUR MONEY MINDSET

Face your fear is the first principle in the book, *The Financial Wisdom of Ebenezer Scrooge: 5 Principles to Transform Your Relationship with Money.* Authored by Rick Kahler and his colleagues, Ted Klontz and Brad Klontz, the book leverages a classic story to teach how financial therapy works to transform our money mindset and ultimately, our behaviors around money. The second principle in the book, explore the past, refers to getting in touch with old memories and the feelings connected to those memories to unlock the prison created by old money scripts. In the book, once Scrooge explored, resolved, and modified his money scripts, he was open to receiving and adopting new ways of being with money. By the end of the book, he was more charitable and generous with his money.

This story is a metaphor for the fact that it is possible to transform a difficult relationship with numbers and dance with them instead. But you have to be ready to discover the root of your money script and make changes to your disruptive and self-sabotaging financial behaviors. That allows you to then take in new information about solutions to improve the financial health of your business and your life.

I recall speaking to a prospective client who wanted advice on how best to manage cash flow. There was a big-time gap between when she received payments from clients and when she needed funds to purchase ingredients to make new product. Her biggest customers were Whole Foods and another major organic/health food grocery. She did not want to lose her shelf space due to inadequate cash on hand to make products and replenish the shelves.

This woman had personal wealth that she'd been using to fund her business, but she was tired of doing so. I suggested getting a working capital line of credit or business loan, and she immediately pushed back. She emphatically said, "I don't want to be in debt! I don't want to owe anybody." The conversation was pretty much over after that. The more I discussed the process and the benefits, the more she shut down and was not receptive to anything else I said.

I prodded a bit and realized her historical relationship and context around money and debt has been traumatic. I wish I had the tools in that moment to unearth and unlock this woman's money scripts around debt. It might have freed her to see how loans from a bank or community development financial institution (CDFI) can be used as a tool to grow her business and take full advantage of that opportunity with Whole Foods.

Interestingly, the money script "debt is bad" is one I've heard from many women owners. I'd love to investigate the source of this belief to draw a reasonable hypothesis, but in the meantime, Luam, the choreographer from Chapter 1, gave me a perspective. "We're afraid to leave our families with a legacy of debt. Debt means failure. We don't see leveraging debt as a positive thing because many of us have only seen debt as a negative thing. We've only seen it used punitively and to take away things in our lives. We've never seen it actually work for something good. I think if we had more examples of that visually, we'd be able to flip it" and use it to build wealth. I see debt as a tool to build a great credit profile (which is critical in the US), to grow my business and generate returns when I'm the lender.

Malika J.'s company offers virtual, board game-centered experiences through their team and enterprise solutions. Her parents migrated to this country from Sri Lanka when her dad pursued a PhD at a major university in Michigan. Malika grew up on a campus with many other international families who were lower/middle class. But she vividly remembers visiting the homes of friends in a higher socioeconomic class who she perceived had more money and a better lifestyle than her own.

Her father impressed an aversion to taking on credit cards and debt on her and her sister. He said the system (capitalism) is set up like a game to keep the poor poor and the rich rich. He told her, "To have a seat at the table, figure out the game and play it. Go to school. Get a good education. Get a job. Don't incur credit card debt, don't buy things that you can't afford." She internalized that and struggled to keep her business going through the pandemic because she did not feel comfortable borrowing money to support it. During our interview, she realized how much her earliest lessons around money are impacting her today. As said earlier, awareness is the first step to transformation. Malika is moving forward despite the struggle, pivoting into a new business, and leveraging other people's money to do so.

Reflect on your own path to entrepreneurship and business ownership. What are your money scripts and trailheads? And how can you flip your script about money?

Smoove through the Triggers

Trigger moments inspire small business owners to take action and remix destructive money scripts because of the share intensity of the pressure or pain caused by a single event or series of events.

From 2006 to 2007, and again during 2013, I was dancing full time and of course had sore muscles, aches, and pains. I tried stretching, foam rollers, lacrosse balls, tiger balm, Icy Hot...anything to relax the muscles. I largely ignored the pain because as I figured dancers, like athletes, endure through the pain. It's like a badge of honor. Eventually, my body gave in, and something snapped or felt stuck. I injured my back, and that pain lasted a long time. The injury was a trigger moment that forced me to change how I took care of my body outside of the dance studio—monthly massages, cleanses, yoga, and Pilates became part of my routine.

For many business owners, the COVID-19 pandemic was a trigger moment that led them to think differently about their businesses. Some got laser focused on offering the products and services they found the most lucrative. Some changed their definition of "office" and allowed their employees to work remotely. Some realized how critical it was to have emergency cash stashed away and have their financial records up to date and ready to apply for funding. Economic downturns and the desire to grow trigger business owners to shift their relationship with money and their numbers to a healthier and positive one. Financial therapists call these moments "interventions." Getting through trigger moments is the third step toward being in flow with your numbers.

After the last two economic downturns, I've seen self-proclaimed non-numbers people give up their limiting money beliefs and behaviors and turn into proficient linguists when it comes to talking about and managing their finances. The trigger moment and transformation seem to happen around or after a business owner has been in business for three years. That's when it happened for Samantha M.

SAMANTHA'S INTERVENTION

Samantha handled general management and ran day-to-day operations while a co-founder with solid experience in financial management oversaw the numbers. When he transitioned out of the company, Samantha was scared. Up to that point, she had not dealt with the finances at all nor had the knowledge to take over that part of the business. She said, "That was an area that started to feel like it was going off in its own orbit, and it felt really unclear and scary to manage." Her only saving grace was that the director of development controlled the company's revenue side of the business and always had his finger on the pulse of when earned revenue from client services or contributed revenue from funders would come in. But once that person also left the company, the safety net was gone.

That was Samantha's trigger moment that made her step up her financial knowledge. She learned about budgeting, revenue drivers, and the risks of underestimating costs. Working in deeper partnership with others in the financial area of the business, Samantha realized that the pricing structure, while idealistic, prevented the company from being able to fund expansion. She was an accidental entrepreneur, who transitioned from life as a creative and a maker (like Chapter 1's Joshua) to that of a founder. She and a friend conceived a business model to decrease the cost of certain services for arts organizations and operate a business at a smaller percentage of income compared to the average nonprofit. Recognizing a real need in the field, they brought the business to life, but it was immediately extremely challenging to grow and shift toward sustainability.

During the pandemic, Samantha became intimately involved in the strategic planning and budgeting of this organization. Samantha is still finding solid footing when it comes to dancing with her numbers. But she does have a more balanced, confident relationship with them than when she started the business. This is very different from what she learned from her parents as a child—that money was a constant hustle and debt was bad. These series of trigger moments led to the shift in Samantha.

RAMON'S INTERVENTION

Ramon R. experienced a similar shift. Ramon is a serial entrepreneur and a sought-after speaker on entrepreneurship, small business, and marketing. He sold two businesses prior to running what is now his fifth business, a marketing agency producing content for large brands. He grew up in a household led by his preacher father, who was a generous and honest man. While he learned charisma, charity, and community-mindedness, not many money lessons were taught in his household. But three businesses and about fifteen years later, he was proud to tell me, "Today, Ramon is debt free, cash flow positive, and has a cash cushion."

For years, Ramon primarily funded his business with credit cards—putting on events, swiping his card, and hoping for the best. That's the American way, right? It seems to be currently, according to the data. In September 2021, Goldman Sachs released a survey revealing that "44 percent of small businesses have less than three months of cash reserves in case of an emergency or another shutdown. Just 31 percent said they were very confident they could access capital if they needed it." The problem is that credit cards are one of the most expensive forms of capital and one of the biggest drains on cash. That's why I encourage clients to get a bank line of credit, which has relatively lower rates than credit cards.

This behavior of funding his business on credit cards continued until eventually, Ramon was tired of being in debt. He knew it was not the best way to operate. But knowing what is right is not enough. Ramon did not change his behavior until a traumatic event happened. He hired a famous speaker for an event, hoping that the headliner would attract a lot of attendees. Ramon put a lot of money on his credit card to cover the cost of the speaker and event, but it did not pan out the way he had hoped. It was a painful experience because he lost a lot of money and realized that while credit card debt is easy to get, it can also follow you for life. Because of the experience, Ramon also learned that it was okay to take on risk as long as you make a return on the money invested (ROI). He said, "If you are paying money to provide a service or product for customers, there should be a direct line to a source of revenue."

This trigger moment set Ramon on a journey to better manage his money. He still professes to not be a numbers person but is grateful to the bookkeeper that taught him how to automate some of his administrative financial activities and use QuickBooks to track his business performance. He was also introduced to a money management system that disciplined his spending habits so that today, he is primarily funding his business with profits and cash reserves instead of credit cards.

At some point during Ramon's life, he developed a bad money script, an unhealthy belief around using debt to fund whatever he couldn't afford to pay with cash. Perhaps he developed a big appetite for taking risks, but he did not balance that with making sure the reward matched the risk. Even after owning multiple businesses for years, it took losing a lot of money and the pressure of living under a lot of debt before he changed his behavior.

As these examples show, entrepreneurship gives you the opportunity to break old money scripts that clutter your mind and change behaviors stunting your growth. However, Wendy Wood, author of *Good Habits, Bad Habits: The Science of Making Positive Changes that Stick*, claims that "standard" interventions like weight-loss programs, public service announcements, and educational programs induce only *short-term* behavior changes. These interventions are good at a) increasing motivation, b) changing people's intentions, c) increasing knowledge and goal-setting strategies to implement, and d) making you feel like you can change but, they do not actually change habits."

Ms. Wood offers three main components of habit-breaking interventions:

§ Cue disruption → Disrupt the cues that trigger an existing habit, leaving room for new habits to form (e.g., to lose weight, make the healthy food easily accessible in the refrigerator or pantry, and make the junk food harder to reach).
§ Environmental reengineering → Add friction to unhealthy behaviors (e.g., add pedestrian walks, bike lanes, and congestion pricing to control traffic in urban areas) and remove friction from healthy behaviors (e.g., institute a bike sharing program).

§ Vigilant monitoring → Repetition is key. Ms. Wood says, "It's easier to maintain the behavior if it's repeated in a specific context."

MICHAEL P.'S INTERVENTION

Wendy Wood's theory about habit-breaking interventions proved true in Michael P.'s situation. Michael P. is the owner of a performance studio that provides personal training, professional athlete consulting, biomechanics, and physical therapy. During our interview, Michael P. shared that before and when he started his business, he was bad at managing money and budgeting. He liked nice things. He loved to take care of his friends and family, and he also had an image and lifestyle that he wanted to maintain. But he admitted that he didn't have the means early on to do so and had to fund his lifestyle with credit card debt.

Michael P. had conflicting money beliefs and behaviors that stemmed from what he learned during childhood. After observing his dad lose a few jobs, he became fearful that if he ever worked for others, at any moment he could be fired and end up with no money. That made him scared to spend cash because he was worried he would lose a job and have none. He also did not like to owe anyone money; it felt stressful and obligatory. However, he used credit cards to fund his lifestyle. It seemed his feelings about credit card debt depended on what it was used for; his need to take care of others and himself overrode his judgment.

These personal habits and behaviors followed him into his adult life, until the moment he lost his job, he lost his apartment and was living in his car (cue disruption). That moment triggered a new practice for Michael P. He started paying for things he *needed* before spending on things he *wanted.* Once he started his entrepreneurial journey (environmental reengineering) as a personal trainer and opened the performance facility with a partner, Michael P. used all the income to build the business, pay rent, and pay down his credit card debt. He never had enough cash to pay himself a decent salary.

He admits that in the beginning, he was afraid of managing money, so he let his partner take care of the financial stuff. When the partnership dissolved and Michael P. flew solo, he tasked the administrative assistant with budgeting him (vigilant monitoring). He told the admin, "If you see anything on the business credit cards or debit card that is not specifically for the business, let me know about it and then shut it down immediately." After doing that for about six months, Michael P.'s impulse purchasing dissipated, and his habit of mismanaging money was broken.

WHEN GROWTH TRIGGERS A MINDSET SHIFT

While economic loss and hardship trigger people to change their money mindset and behaviors, the desire to grow and succeed does, too. Vivian is a former corporate marketing manager turned start-up founder of a professional social network that enables companies to build relationships with women and diverse professionals. She had lofty goals of people buying into her vision and readily joining the magical journey of entrepreneurship with her. She is a Wharton

School alumna with a background in finance, so she felt confident about her numbers.

She had not been in business for a year before the 2020 global pandemic hit. She thought about shutting down her company, but ultimately decided to give herself three months to make it work. Her business focus was on getting traction and making money, but she had old limiting beliefs that limited the business's full growth potential. Vivian is an immigrant from China and as she tells it, "Being Asian, I've never had a single penny of debt, so the idea of putting debt on my credit card to start a business was extremely scary to me. So I did the only thing that I knew how to do...work many hours and jobs and hustle to fund the business myself."

Vivian is very proud of how scrappy she is, making do with little, reinvesting every penny into the business, and getting traction in her business faster than is expected of a pre-seed company. When she recommitted herself to her business in 2020, she debated investing in various software costing thousands of dollars. Her old money mindset would have said, "You don't need to spend thousands of dollars, you could probably do a lot of the work this software does or you can find an intern to do X, Y, Z tasks." Ultimately, Vivian decided to buy the software and said to herself, "You deserve this. You deserve the respect to invest in yourself and your business so that you can have outsized outcomes." Within a month of buying the software, Vivian recouped her investment and realized she needed to get out of the "penny-pinching immigrant mentality" and start respecting herself. She said, "Because if I didn't respect myself, how are these investors going to see me as an investment worthy of putting dollars behind?"

THE JOURNEY TO CHANGE

Vivian's trigger moment happened after just one year in business, possibly because she was already questioning her belief systems formed as a child in China and the US, and contemplating change. According to the Stages of Change or Transtheoretical Model introduced in the late 1970s by researchers James Prochaska and Carlo DiClemente, the six stages of behavior change are:

1. Precontemplation: Denial that a behavior is damaging and ignorance about the consequences of your actions.
2. Contemplation: Having conflicting emotions about changing behavior yet more awareness of the potential benefits of change.
3. Preparation: Experimentation with small changes and information gathering on how to change a behavior.
4. Action: Once someone has taken time in the prior three steps, they are likely ready to take direct action toward a goal.
5. Maintenance: At this stage, it is important to avoid temptation and continue reinforcing the new habit.
6. Relapse: This is common throughout every step, but the key to overcoming a relapse is not undermining your self-confidence. Reassess the techniques, actions, and rewards you've set up to maintain the new behavior and stay motivated.

Joe A., a marketing agency owner and LinkedIn strategist, has been proactive for years in shifting his old money habits and behaviors. His mom was an entrepreneur who was unfortunately always in debt, financing her business and life on credit cards; but she would also spend conservatively and look for deals. Joe's dad was more apathetic about money and worked a lot of entry-level jobs. Joe remembered they could not afford to pay for things he needed, like a computer for school.

He was frustrated as a child about a lack of money in the household, and he grew up thinking that money was a gift from God bestowed on the lucky people. When his mother bought him and his siblings lottery tickets, Joe wrote down all the things he would buy, should he be lucky to win. He thought he was an unlucky person but that if he worked hard, perhaps he would get lucky. He started his business with this mindset, made his own way, and became financially independent.

His experience as an entrepreneur triggered a change in his money belief. After being in business for a few years, he realized making money was not about luck; it was about having a good strategy. Yet Joe still struggled with a self-limiting belief that he was not good at understanding the numbers. Therefore, he relapsed a couple of times into old, unhealthy money behaviors. For example, he completely deferred to his partner on all financial matters, but the partner turned out to be like Joe's mom in that the partner was not good at managing credit.

A trigger moment occurred when the business had strong six- or seven-figure sales, but the partners were running out of cash and took in investor money. At that time, Joe remembered, "I still didn't understand the money. I was always scared. That moment was a scary moment." That was also the final straw for him because after that, he went on a journey to really take control of his numbers and understand them.

Joe completely changed his behavior and his head talk. He invested in coaches, workshops, business communities, and various resources to build that financial muscle. He started telling himself, "I am a money person. I understand money. I understand the profit and loss statement. I understand the cost of goods and profit. I understand the different elements of the balance sheet and the balance between making profits and having cash." With a stronger command of his numbers, Joe has been able to grow his first business to the status of 178 on the Inc. 500 list.

After speaking to other business owners like Samantha, Ramon, Michael P., and Joe, who do not consider themselves numbers people, I truly believe that it is possible for all business owners to take control of their numbers and engage in an easier relationship with them. However, it starts by becoming aware that unhealthy money scripts exist, then rescripting old money mindsets ingrained from childhood, being open to the invitation to dance with our numbers, and acting on the trigger moments that this entrepreneurial journey provides. Once that has taken place, your minds will be open and receptive to learn and implement financial management best practices.

SECTION 2

STRENGTHEN

Build Your Core

A dance teacher introduced me to Pilates to help overcome dance injuries and to warm my body before rehearsals. I was such a Pilates enthusiast that I became a certified instructor teaching at Equinox and other private studios in New York. Pilates is a low-impact, high-intensity exercise that improves body strength, flexibility, and alignment with a focus on building core strength. Before every single rehearsal and performance, I run through a series of Pilates exercises to prepare my body for the intensity. There is no way I'd be able to perform at a professional level as someone over forty years old, if it was not for having a strong core, which supports all other parts of my body.

In the same way that dancers must strengthen their physical core to be at peak performance, business owners must strengthen their financial core to grow to peak performance. When your numbers, financial team, and operations (the financial core) are strong, the success of the business will be long lived and you will be able to choreograph the life you want. Clients who engage our CFO services and work with our financial choreographers have been out of flow with their numbers. They're ready and eager to improve their financial position but often don't know where to start. CEOs have said:

"I don't know how my business is performing but for my peace of mind and sanity, I want to get a grip on my financials (what's going in and coming out)."

"I want to increase employee salaries, offer benefits, and pay myself more, but I don't know how we can afford it."

"We need to tighten up our systems and have a better structure when it comes to the financials."

"I need someone to hold my hand and help me make good decisions for the future."

"We need to create financial projections or a budget and set targets to meet the goals."

Do any of these issues and goals resonate with you?

If you're ready to get right with your numbers, take these actions to strengthen your financial core:

§ Actively manage cash flow
§ Be performance driven

§ Build business credit

§ Reduce risk with systems, processes and controls

§ Plan for the future

Some of these lessons will be familiar and some will be new. Overall, my hope is that your mind is open to receiving these lessons and you truly take the time to work on this part of your business.

ACTIVELY MANAGE CASH FLOW

Have you ever been excited to reach or surpass a sales goal but wondered where the cash is to show for it? A start-up showing traction in terms of customer demand and a highly profitable company with double-digit, year-over-year growth can both run out of cash if it isn't actively managed. Without an intentional focus on measuring and growing cash flow, as well as profit, companies risk failure. Thus, the saying,

"Revenue is vanity, profit is sanity, but cash is reality."

According to a September 2019 report by the US Small Business Administration's Office of Advocacy, about half of all small businesses survive five years or longer. About one-third of [small businesses] survive ten years or longer. They cited various reasons for this failure rate including no demand due to poor understanding of customer needs, unsustainable growth, ineffective business planning, and inadequate management. But the number-one reason small businesses fail is they run out of cash (CB Insights, 2021).

Cash is the life force energy flowing through every business, keeping it strong, agile, and alive. Positive cash flow indicates that more cash is flowing into the business from operations, funding, and investment sources than is flowing out. It does not mean that the business is profitable. Negative cash flow means that the business is burning (paying expenses, repaying debt, paying owners and investors) or churning more money than it's taking in. Negative cash flow is not equivalent to experiencing a net loss. I'll explain more a little later.

Arijit, serial entrepreneur and current CEO of an artificial intelligence company, said startups should make sure they never run out cash. He said, "Nobody cares if according to your books, the business looks profitable. If you run out of cash, you're dead. You don't get to play; the game is over." In his business, he made sure he had enough cash for a period of time such that he could pivot and fix one catastrophic mistake. If economic conditions were bad, he wanted to have enough cash and runway to be able to fix two catastrophic mistakes. This was crucial during the pandemic because he was able to keep all of his employees. While I believe a business should have three to six months of cash saved in case of emergency, Arijit believes the amount saved depends on how your company is doing and how well the business owner is at pivoting and getting the business out of cash crunches.

To control cash flow, timing is key! A good rule of thumb is to accelerate cash flowing into the business and delay when cash flows out of the business. This is easier said than done because business owners often don't realize they are leaking cash until suddenly, they can't make payroll or meet their debt obligations, which leads to unhappy employees, credit and credibility issues and stressed-out CEOs. Keep a finger on the pulse of your business's cash position by creating a simple forecast of what's coming in and what's going out weeks or months in advance. This is one of my Ten Cash Commandments to increase cash flow and general business health.

1. ***Don't confuse profits with extra cash.*** These are two very different concepts that are often confused. Revenue is money earned, not just cash collected. Expenses are costs incurred, not just cash flowing out. If revenue is $400,000 ($300,000 in cash received from sales + $100,000 in unpaid invoices) and expenses are $200,000 ($125,000 in cash spent on operations + $50,000 in unpaid bills + $25,000 in expenses charged to a credit card), the difference between net profit and net cash available is:

Column 1	Column 2
Income Statement	**Statement of Cash flow**
Revenue = $400,000	Cash received = $300,000
Expenses = $200,000	Cash spent on operations = $125,000
Net Profit = $200,000	***Net cash flow available = $175,000***

Profits increase the value of your business and signal to lenders and investors that your business is fiscally healthy. But if you want to increase cash flow from operations, adjust the profit levers (increase volume, increase price, reduce cash spent on direct costs and overhead expenses), reduce accounts receivable days, and increase accounts payable days.

2. ***Reduce accounts receivable days.*** Receivables or unpaid invoices are the easiest sources of cash. To shorten the

amount of time it takes to turn these into cash, 1) enforce payment terms and spell out the ramifications of late payment; 2) offer clients payment plans with deadlines for each payment; 3) offer slight discounts for early payment and payments via ACH; and most importantly, communicate with the client. Set up auto invoice reminders because perhaps they simply forgot to pay. If you don't feel comfortable pressing clients for payment and don't want to risk losing the relationship, have an external party like an outsourced CFO handle collections. The worst-case scenario is that the client plays hard to get, in which case have a lawyer send a demand letter. I had an IT services client do that, and the customer who had been giving him the runaround for a year finally got on the phone (albeit reluctantly) to strike a deal.

3. ***Manage direct supplier and labor costs.*** Review the fees and scope of services annually with vendors and contractors to make sure you're paying for what you truly need. If market or internal conditions call for you to reduce costs, communicate with vendors right away to see if there's anything they are willing to do like reduce fees for a certain time, reduce the scope, put you on a payment plan, or extend your business trade credit. Don't avoid payments or ignore calls; it will affect your reputation and business credit. Always have at least three alternative vendors and contractors on standby to avoid operational disruptions if the current supplier and contractor relationship doesn't work out.

4. ***Audit operating expenses quarterly or semiannually.*** The easiest places to reduce or cut costs are unused subscriptions, travel, office expenses (excluding rent), meals, and some insurance costs. Also, keep tight controls around

employee reimbursements. Set a spending limit on company credit cards issued to employees. Have clearly stated policies and procedures around what expenses are reimbursable and which are not, and have employees sign an agreement acknowledging their responsibility for using company funds.

5. ***Hire slow and fire fast.*** This goes for employees and contractors. People costs are the biggest sources of cash leaks since it's the largest expense for most businesses. One way businesses leak cash here is by hiring the wrong employee for a position. The employee will likely spend more time getting up to speed and trying to fit into the role than being productive. High turnover also puts a drain on cash because of the time taken to recruit, interview and train talent before reaping any return on investment. To avoid this cash leak, follow the adage, "Hire slow and fire fast." When someone is not performing well, have a conversation with them to try and identify the source of the problem. If you determine that they would be a better fit in another position within the company, set them up for success there. Finally, create a culture and environment that promotes high productivity where employees are happy to work because you are providing what they value, whether it's the type of work, benefits offered, autonomy, fun, or camaraderie.

6. ***Manage the flow of inventory (inventory days).*** Cash gets stuck in inventory if you order the same product from too many suppliers, keep old inventory for too long, and demand is low. Use an inventory management system to track the inventory turnover rate or how quickly inventory is purchased and sold. A low inventory turnover ratio indicates that inventory is not turning into cash

fast enough, and therefore cash is figuratively stuck on the shelf. Annually do a physical inventory to identify which items aren't selling and move them to clearance or bundle them with more popular items.

7. ***Invest in high-return marketing activities to increase sales volume.*** Marketing can really suck up cash if you let it. While it may take at least six months for marketing efforts to show some dividends, clearly define with a marketing specialist the strategy, goals of the marketing efforts, and what success looks like in terms of numbers (e.g., X number of followers, Y number of clients, Z number of unique impressions or visitors). If the marketing efforts are not showing increasing ROI within a reasonable time, rethink the marketing plan so money is not wasted. Do a little research to find out how long it should take to see a return on marketing dollars on your campaign.

8. ***Raise prices.*** Even if you increase it by 1 percent or 5 percent, raising prices is the quickest and most underused way to increase revenue and cash flow, but business owners are scared to do it. I don't suggest making drastic changes or doing this frequently, but at least make sure your prices are comparable to those of competitors, reflect what customers are willing to pay for results, and factor in your worth (expertise, experience, networks, etc.). An outsourced CFO or financial consultant can help you determine the optimal revenue (price and volume) to cover your business's cash needs. If you want to start working on this, in Chapter 6 I break down how to strategically think about pricing.

9. ***Stay liquid.*** Cash flows like water. Build a cash stash of three to six months of operating expenses or have ready

access to capital. Don't know how much to save? First, track how much the business burns through in cash monthly on average. While credit cards are available to fund cash shortfalls, the interest rate on a business loan or line of credit are considerably better than that of a credit card. Apply for a line of credit before you need it. Banks and alternative lenders prefer to lend to businesses with profits and consistent cash flow, not those scrounging for money. Always have the following information ready to discuss with lenders: two years of business tax returns, a current income statement and balance sheet, a breakdown of your current debt obligations and future business plans or projections. Most importantly, keep your personal and business credit profile and score strong.

10. ***Growth sucks cash; plan accordingly.*** Many of us think of an idea for growth or scale but don't consider what it takes to bring that idea to fruition. To avoid cash shortfalls by growing faster than you can afford to, build a cash forecast. First, have a clear plan around the product or service that will grow or scale the business and specific client that needs that offering. Quantify in dollars any additional investments (people, technology, space, expertise, assets) needed to bring this offering center stage. Then, look back a year or so and identify trends in your current cash flow; most importantly, know how much cash you typically burn. Finally, look forward six to twelve weeks in advance, and align when you think money is going to come into the business and when money is going to flow out of the business to cover the cost of current business operations and the cost of investments in growth. If you foresee running out of cash in future weeks, start looking at all viable funding options now.

BE PERFORMANCE DRIVEN

The financial health of a business is measured based on its liquidity (the ability to keep cash flowing in), profitability (the percentage of revenue available to reinvest in growth), and solvency (the ability to pay one's debt). Financial metrics are one set of data points that can be used to measure business performance, but there are many others. By tracking business performance on a regular basis, you will gain insights into the business's areas of strength and weakness and be able to make informed decisions quickly. If you do not currently track performance beyond looking at your bank account, start small by selecting five to ten simple numbers to track weekly. Think about the financial, sales, marketing, employee performance, or even operational metrics that can help you keep a pulse on what's going on in your business (e.g., revenue by product/customer, gross profit margin, project hours by employee, number of days to collect customer payments, number of customers completing online orders as a percent of total web visitors, customer satisfaction).

Use the data points you've selected (also known as key performance metrics) as a way to "cut through all the feelings, opinions, and egos and boil [your] organization down to a handful of objective numbers that give you an absolute pulse on where things are" (Wickman, 2011). The key is to be consistent with tracking these numbers especially if you are not in the habit of monitoring performance through your accounting system. In fact, tie each number to a person's role in the company so they are responsible for reporting that number weekly and implementing solutions when the number is off.

If you have a consulting business, measure the amount of time employees spend weekly on client work (billable hours) as a percentage of their total weekly working hours. This measurement is called capacity utilization, and it's useful in assessing the employees' operational efficiency and in determining whether you are charging enough for that service. A consistently high utilization rate means that employees are overworked, and you need to increase the client's pricing to cover the cost of an additional employee working on that account. A low utilization rate means that your employees need more work.

Product-based companies should track inventory turnover ratio, which is the rate at which inventory is produced and turned into revenue. A low ratio implies weak sales and signals that either something is wrong with the product, marketing is ineffective, or there's a change in customer demand. If the items in inventory aren't sold, cash will not be available to meet the company's obligations.

If you sell primarily online, measure the percentage of website visitors that click to cart, and how many visitors actually complete purchase so you can figure out where along the path, from initial visit to purchase, potential customers, and therefore potential revenue gets stuck. By tracking this information, you will know where along the sales funnel to concentrate your efforts to increase customer conversion.

One number that should be on every business owner's dashboard or scorecard is the monthly cash burn rate—the average amount of cash spent monthly on operations, repaying debt, investing in assets, and paying owners. Surprisingly, it cannot be easily tracked in an accounting software like QuickBooks or Xero. I maintain it on a spreadsheet for clients.

You can track financial performance metrics in a reliable accounting software like QuickBooks, Xero, FreshBooks, NetSuite, and Intacct if the financial records are up to date, accurate, and categorized in compliance with accounting standards. Hire a bookkeeper that knows accounting principles, not just an accounting software, to do the books monthly. Have them adjust the chart of accounts and the accounting system so transactions are categorized correctly, and the reports are reflective of your business. If needed, use third-party Fintech systems (like Bill.com, Melio, Expensify, Harvest, Shopify, PayPal, etc.) that integrate into your accounting system so that all financial information is seamlessly captured in one place. Have your bookkeeper check all systems periodically to make sure they are working and feeding numbers correctly into your accounting software.

Every month pull down and review financial reports in the accounting software so you know how your business is performing at any moment. A business adviser once told me that my responsibility as a CEO is to hire people to do 80 percent of the work but always keep oversight of about 20 percent of the work. Keep your finger on the pulse of every aspect of your business, even the areas that make you uncomfortable. The three most familiar financial reports are the income statement, known as "Profit and Loss," the balance sheet, and the cash flow statement. To get the most intel out of these reports and others, have your financial manager (typically a CFO) analyze them and tell you the story behind the numbers so you can make strategic decisions to improve the financial well-being of the company.

If you only have the books updated and reviewed once a year for tax purposes, you will not be able to make timely, data-driven decisions for your business. Gut instinct, intuition, and sheer sales savvy will take your business to a certain point, but as your business gets more complex and financial issues arise, you will need to analyze the numbers for answers or get help doing so. If the books are kept at your CPA's office, request a monthly review of the numbers to hold the CPA accountable for keeping the books up to date and, most importantly, so you know how your business is performing and can fix any problems.

Tammy and her husband own an organic hair and beauty products company. When Tammy hired us, she said, "We have grown so much in sales over the past two years, but we never have enough cash in the bank to pay ourselves or buy ingredients in bulk to take advantage of discounts. What do we do?" Tammy had a great bookkeeper keeping the financial records organized in QuickBooks, so we were able to rely on the financial statements and analyze the numbers looking for potential areas where cash was leaking out of the business.

The income statement told us that the company was slightly profitable over the past two years in that the income received covered the cost of production and running the business. In fact, the company operated pretty lean, but the profits were not enough to pay the owners a decent salary. The balance sheet showed that the company barely had enough assets (e.g., cash, inventory on hand, fixed assets) to cover its liabilities (what they owed to vendors and lenders). The cash flow statement reflected the same story Tammy told us. After doing more forensic analysis, I realized the reasons Tammy's company was losing money was that she was: 1) making products that had negative profitability; 2) spending money across four costly initiatives at the same time—production, packaging, shipping/handling and marketing; and 3) creating new product lines instead of leveraging the products and customer loyalty (assets) they already had to generate revenue in other ways with little cash investment.

Tammy, like many business owners, did not really understand the cost of growth and how it was negatively impacting her bank account. But because she had reliable historical data, we were able to analyze the financial reports from the accounting system, give Tammy insight into her business's performance, identify the source of financial issues, and quickly put together a plan to resolve it. Tammy followed that plan and cut the products that generated no profit and found a shared kitchen to mass produce their home-grown products more cost effectively. With our help, she also secured a line of credit to help pay down some debt and order enough ingredients and supplies to fill back orders and build up a little stash of product inventory. Have your accounting or financial person review the numbers at least monthly, identify problems or potential risks to the business, and help you strategize on how to improve the financial health of your business. I bet you will sleep better at night and have the mental freedom to focus on other things like business development, employee satisfaction, and remaining competitive.

CHAPTER 5

Fortify Your Core

Consistency is required to be a top performer. Performers and athletes know that muscles need repetition before they are ready for the main stage. When performance day arrives, your mind and body are on autopilot. The adrenaline just kicks all of that preparation and repetitive training into high gear. Likewise, good cash flow management requires consistency. Tracking and monitoring business performance takes consistency. Once you're in flow with the rhythm of your numbers, you'll feel a sense of control, ease, and confidence over your business. What also requires consistency in business is building credit and efficiently running operations.

BUILD BUSINESS CREDIT

According to Carolyn, a SCORE mentor, "The top three things business owners need funding for are: 1) opening a new location after being successful with the first one; 2) marketing in the hopes of driving business sales which business owners almost never get money for; and 3) a line extension (e.g., a spa owner who wants to sell a product)." Carolyn is of the opinion that most business owners don't need to borrow money to fund growth if they "make haste slowly." She believes owners should focus on generating revenue by starting with smaller growth efforts, building stage by stage until the success of a new location, line extension, or some other growth idea is proven and successful.

Want to launch a new product? Launch it to existing customers first to test interest and learn what customers like about the new product. To access a new customer segment, partner with another business already entrenched in that market. If you are a service-based business launching a branded line of product (e.g., a beauty salon launching shampoos and conditioners), know that a product-based business is a very different business model. Start small by manufacturing a limited run for your VIP customers or Instagram followers. Carolyn said that "business owners often hate this approach because to look professional, they think they need to have their brand on thousands of bottles on a shelf and have all the affiliated products with it. But they fail to realize how little revenue a new product or idea might make early on. If they just started with one hundred bottles of one product, they can test the market and financial viability of it without investing so much time and money."

So credit cards become the source of funding for growth, which has its pros and cons. The downside to funding growth with credit cards is that if you don't make enough money quickly from a new venture, you'll be at risk of losing cash fast. If the new venture proves successful, you would have not only banked on yourself but also been able to repay the credit card, thus building your credit profile. Business credit cards are typically the first source of funding for many small business owners and the first opportunity you get to build good business credit. Stay below the credit limit, pay on time, and pay more than the minimum required.

If you give employees corporate cards, set a spending a limit on their card and have their manager and/or your book-keeper review the credit card statements for extraordinary expenses. Take these steps to protect your credit profile since your ability as a business owner to access credit is initially tied to your personal credit. Since credit cards are often the most expensive form of funding, have a lower-cost form of financing available to take up the slack if necessary. A line of credit typically has a lower interest rate, and you can draw on it whenever necessary.

Even if business is doing well and there is enough income to cover your business's cash needs, it is still a good practice to have a line of credit. In fact, banks prefer to lend to businesses that are financially stable, show that they have credit and are responsible with it. If you don't currently have a line of credit, apply for it if you can, even if you don't need it right now. If you don't draw on the credit line, you wouldn't owe the lender anything. But if you need access to capital in a pinch, it's there. If the 2009 recession and COVID-19 pandemic have taught us nothing else, it is to have funding that covers at least six months of expenses, squared away, in case of emergencies. A line of credit can serve as "just-in-case money."

One of our clients owned a bakery. They kept maxing out their credit cards in order to fund ingredients, supplies, etc. in advance of receiving sales. If their oven or freezer broke down, they would have had no funds to buy another one, so I recommended they apply for a line of credit from the bank they have had a relationship with for years. Thankfully, they were approved and now they have relatively less expensive funding to support them.

Before asking for credit, know:

§ how much you need;
§ when you need it;
§ what you are going to spend it on—day-to-day expenses, construction on a new building, growth, etc.; and
§ how you plan to pay it back.

Your business type and activities will also affect the funding available for your business. A truck is financed differently from commercial real estate. Medical practices and companies with valuable assets (equipment, long-term contracts, receivables) tend to receive better financing than other companies. Funding sources include SBA loans, traditional loans, term loans (e.g., Kabbage, OnDeck), merchant cash advances (e.g., Square Capital, Shopify capital loans), supplier credit lines, accounts receivable factoring, traditional and investment crowd funding (e.g., KIVA, Indiegogo, Regulation CF, Regulation D). Each type of funding has pros and cons, so work with a financial expert and lender to see which options are best for your business. The biggest upside to taking on these sources of funding is that it can help you build business credit.

Business credit, like personal credit, is built over time. As you build your business's credit profile, you will get access to higher credit limits, better terms, and lower interest rates. Your business credit profile can also affect your ability to qualify for contracts, raise money and purchase assets needed to operate, and boost your business's value. Credit profiles and credit scores are created when vendors, suppliers, or creditors report your business's activity and payment history to business credit bureaus like Dun & Bradstreet, Equifax, and Experian.

Establish credit by setting up a federal employer ID number, business phone line, business bank account, and registered Dun & Bradstreet D-U-N-S number under your company's legal name. If you are registered as a sole proprietor for tax purposes, incorporate your business or form a limited liability company so your business's credit can be established separate from your own. Refer to your CPA and lawyer for professional advice on the best entity for you, even if you have been in business for years. The credit bureaus use these pieces of information as well as vendor and lender reports of payment history, public records, legal filings, etc. to build your company's credit profile.

To build business credit: (DeNicola, 2022)

§ Check your business credit reports and scores (e.g., Dun & Bradstreet PAYDEX score) from all three credit bureaus to see what your current status is and clear up any discrepancies. There is typically a fee to retrieve business credit reports unlike personal credit reports.
§ Use a business credit card and other vendor credit cards (especially Net 30 cards) that report payment to at least three of the business credit bureaus.
§ Pay on time and more than the minimum. Your credit score may bump up even higher if you pay earlier than the due date.
§ Keep monitoring your credit report to remove discrepancies.

By taking these steps, over time you will be able to access financing based on your business credit instead of your personal credit.

REDUCE RISK WITH SYSTEMS, PROCESSES, AND CONTROLS

I thought I had met my match with reducing financial risk when I met Anthony C. He owns a seven-figure IT services company. He had a bookkeeper who did everything: invoicing, collections, bank deposits, bank transfers, reviewing timesheets, submitting payroll, bill payment, and bookkeeping. The only thing she didn't do was sign checks and approve payroll. Payroll was a pretty manual process in that employees wrote their times into logbooks. A supervisor would review and sign off on the timesheets and submit it to the bookkeeper who would, in turn, tabulate and manually enter times into a payroll system for processing.

That process left a lot of room for human error and fraud, which did occur. Anthony C. was disappointed because he wholeheartedly trusted his bookkeeper who was part of his business family for ten years. On top of this, Anthony received a notice from the IRS with a bill for thousands in back taxes plus penalties and interest for some other alleged infraction. He was furious but, at the same time, hopeful we would bring better oversight to his financial operations because he did not have the time nor expertise to do so.

We helped Anthony recruit a new bookkeeper, check the person's references, and did a full background check. The bookkeeper's activities were limited to financial record keeping, invoicing, and administrative tasks. We reviewed the books monthly, managed collections, performed all bank and cash management activities, and approved payroll. The client also moved to another payroll service that had time tracking systems fully integrated into the payroll system, leaving little to no room for human error or fraud.

Businesses with one person managing the entire financial operations are susceptible to the same risk. To avoid these issues and save time, money, and headaches, hire a controller or outsourced CFO to oversee the bookkeeping and all of your accounting and financial operations. If you have a manufacturing, construction, or general contractor business, it's best to hire a controller. Otherwise, an outsourced CFO is right for the job. I clarify the difference between both the various accounting and finance roles in Chapter 7.

These are a few of the important systems to have as part of your financial operations. The more integrated these systems are, the smoother your financial operations will run, the lower the risk of error and the more time you and your financial team have to spend increasing your company's profits and value.

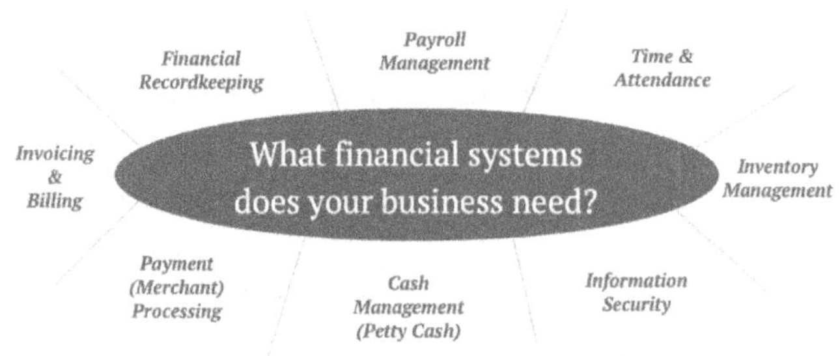

Sophie runs an animal shelter, and every evening she leaves some starting cash in a lock box in the office for the receptionist to start the cash register for the day. The shelter makes money from animal adoption fees, donations, pet training/ grooming, and a small pet supplies shop. The receptionist manages the small pet supplies shop set up near her desk. Every morning she logs the date and amount of starting cash under her name in the point-of-sale system. Before leaving for the day, she closes out the cash register, prints and signs a report with the day's purchases, refunds, and starting and ending cash, and then puts them all into a lock box with the remaining cash. Once a week, the bookkeeper tallies up the daily reports to make sure the income reported by the point-of-sale system is the same amount that hit the bank account. This is a great example of what it means to have checks and balances because the bookkeeper verifies what the receptionist reported. And then Sophie, the owner, can log into her point-of-sale (POS) or accounting system and track the activity as well.

Here are a few other important controls to put in place to keep your business safeguarded.

§ Run a background check on everyone managing financial activities.
§ Sign your checks. Use the electronic signature and signature stamp sparingly.
§ Put spending limits on employee credit cards.
§ Document the steps your financial department takes to manage all the accounting and financial processes. Work with your financial team to create a list of steps and tasks to be completed weekly, monthly, etc. (for invoicing, bill pay, payroll, sales tax, bookkeeping).
§ Include a set of rules to be followed when performing any financial activities and handling any of the financial systems including who should be the primary and back-up person for each task.

These "rules of engagement" will save you time, money, and headache by reducing the financial risk in your business. You will also be glad you documented the processes especially if that bookkeeper who has been handling the business's money matters for years, suddenly decides to quit or terminate your agreement. At least you'll have something to help transition the next hire into the role.

CHAPTER 6

Move from Your Core

A goal without a plan is a wish. When I'm rehearsing for a long performance run (for example, six or eight shows in week), I dance full out in the rehearsal studio as if I were on stage or I at least go hard 75 percent of the time. That's because I want to get a feel for the moments when I go 100 percent, the moments I can pull back, the moments I can breathe in the movement, and the moments I need to power through. Don't get me wrong; I enjoy every minute of performing, but it is an intense workout. I can't just get on the stage and run on passion and euphoria because when muscles are sore and energy is running on fumes, I need a plan to get to the end of the piece and the end of the performance run successfully. Olympians often talk about how they plan and strategize so they can run their own race to the goal line.

Sonya K. and her partner operated an acupuncture practice for six years. In that time, they grew a loyal following, bought a space in the city, which is a huge achievement, and started renting out rooms in their commercial space to other freelance wellness professionals to complement their services. When I initially met Sonya, I asked, "What is your one-year revenue goal?" After she gave me a number, I followed up with, "How do you plan to get there?" to which she responded, "I'm not sure. That's why I'm here to get your help to figure that out."

PLAN FOR THE FUTURE

The fifth action small business owners should take to strengthen their financial core is to plan for the future. Start with a one-year goal and build from there. Before helping Sonya K. with the planning, I asked, "Why is achieving this financial goal so important? What would it mean for your business?"

She wanted to be able to afford hiring more people, give higher wages and benefits to the people she already employed, and pay herself a comfortable wage. To achieve her business and personal goals, Sonya, like many other business owners, needs not just more revenue but more profits. Using a mathematical equation, I showed her that what the business was currently generating was not enough to cover general operations far less cover growth. By doing the math, she could clearly see that she needed to make changes to scale the business. Math removed any hesitation or resistance to my suggestions.

Profit is the revenue left over after all expenses are paid; it's what remains available to reinvest in the growth of the business. Take the six steps Sonya and other clients have taken to devise a plan for generating more profits in twelve to twenty-four months. Creating a business plan can seem like a daunting and complex process because it requires a lot of research and forces you to imagine what your business would look like in the future in terms of marketing, sales, operations, production, people. It's difficult to see past what you're doing now. But with a guided process and a focus on only twelve to twenty-four months into the future, I'm simplifying that process with these steps and supporting growth minded business owners on their path to financial freedom. Learn more about the path here: https://fincorestrong.com/sales/.

PUT YOURSELF FIRST

This is the biggest decision that most business owners do not make. Usually, we think about businesses like an income statement—focused on driving revenue and prioritizing all the people we have to pay, especially employees. We often treat ourselves as an afterthought, basing our salaries and take-home pay on whatever profits are left over. But if you start with your desired salary and add the full cost of running your business, you will determine the minimum revenue and profits your business needs to make to cover everything. If you've ever felt guilt or doubt around giving yourself a raise, doing this calculation will help shift your mindset and release those emotions. It will also help validate if the one-year revenue and profit goal you imagined is realistic.

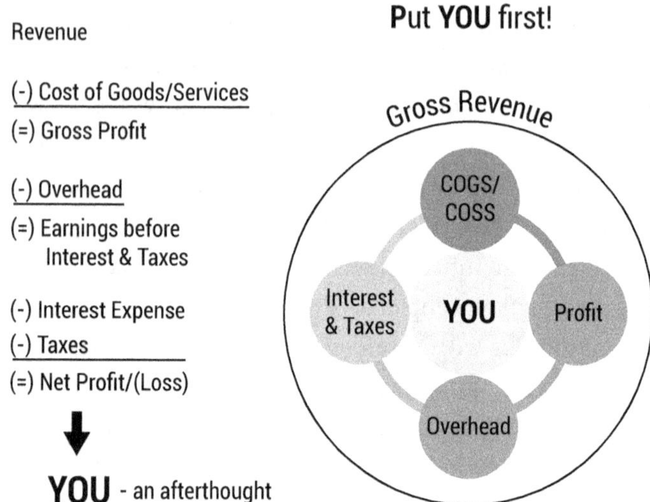

REVIEW THE PAST

Use historical data and information as a starting point for building your growth plan. Look at financial reports as well as bank and credit card statements for the past few years to identify trends in cash flow, income, and spending month to month to get a sense of your business performance. Assume most expenses would stay the same for another year or two. Once you've decided how you will grow the business, research and make reasonable assumptions around how much more it will cost in production, operations, marketing, people, technology, etc. This brings me to the next point.

OUTLINE THE PATH FORWARD THROUGH INNOVATION.

If you want to get to the next level in your business, make more money and profits, then you've got to do something different. As a professional dancer, my creative juices are always percolating. All business owners should make space to live in visionary and ABC (Always Be Creating) mode. I'm most creative and inspired in the morning, in the shower or after a workout. Wherever you find inspiration, schedule time to be in that space monthly or quarterly to visualize the future and come up with ideas on how to expand your business.

Visualization leads to creative thinking and big ideas. Innovation is the execution and implementation of a creative idea; it's the creation of something new that can lead to new opportunities, a competitive advantage, and additional revenue for your business. G. Shawn Hunter, author of *Out Think: How Innovative Leaders Drive Exceptional Outcome*, is quoted saying, "Innovation isn't a mysterious black box, it can be simple small tweaks to exciting processes, products or interactions" (Peek, 2021). Making simple small tweaks that provide customers with a better solution to their problem or pain, will positively impact your bottom line.

There are ten types of innovation—new opportunities to increase revenue and profits beyond creating a new product or service—according to in-depth research by Doblin, an innovation-focused firm owned by Deloitte (Doblin, 2015). The ten types are:

1. Profit model—how your business makes money
2. Network—how you connect with others to create value
3. Structure—how you organize and align your talent an assets
4. Process—how you use signature or superior methods to do your work

5. Product performance—how you develop distinguishing features and functionality
6. Product system—how you create complementary products and services
7. Service—how you support and amplify the value of your offerings
8. Channel—how you deliver your offerings to customers and users
9. Brand—how you represent your offerings and business
10. Customer engagement—how you foster compelling interactions

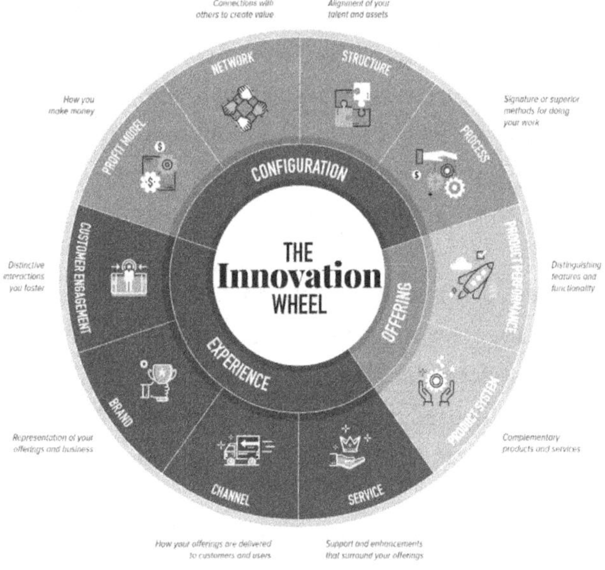

The content is borrowed from: www.visualcapitalist.com

Since 2007, Jennie D. has owned a certified organic ice cream company selling ice cream retail in a brick-and-mortar scoop shop in Brooklyn, by the pint in Whole Foods and other health food groceries, as well as wholesale to restaurants. Around her tenth year in business, Jennie D. realized the business was losing a lot of money, so she did a deep dive analysis of every distribution channel and every customer account. She learned that distributing pints out of state was not profitable for the business.

The sales volume for out-of-state customers was not high enough to fill a truck and cover the costs of freight, transportation, and everything else that went into the cost of that distribution channel. Therefore, Jennie cut unprofitable out-of-state customers, got rid of the commercial truck (and all the costs associated with it), and instead, hired a distributor to transport pints to customers. While her business lost revenue, she cut expenses, gained profitability, and achieved double-digit margins, which is higher than industry average.

When the 2020 pandemic hit and decimated the wholesale side of her business, Jennie went into action again, quickly pivoting by taking advantage of lower commercial rents in the city. She used financing and funds from the first store to open two more retail scoop stores in the city. She also used price as a lever and increased the price per scoop of ice cream. While having three retail locations is physically difficult to manage, Jennie keeps her eye keenly on her numbers measuring everything down to the impact of sample tastings on labor costs. Jennie runs a lean operation today and is now focused on sustaining her profit margins.

The 4 Ps

The right innovation for your business should fit four criteria.
It should 1) alleviate a *pain* or solve a *problem* for your current
or a new client; 2) show promise of being *profitable*; 3) *play*
to your business's strengths; and 4) align with your *passions*.
Take the following actions and ask yourself the following
questions to decide the right innovation(s) for you.

1. Alleviate pain or solve problem: Interview current clients
   and prospects to identify what they really need right now
   in their own words. Consider what current events has
   or can change their needs. Read industry reports to see
   what new trends are popping up in your industry and the
   industries of direct and indirect competitors. If you have
   a bakery, an indirect competitor would be an ice cream
   company or a company selling make it yourself cookies.
2. Promise of profitability: What is the demand for the *new*
   innovation? What market share is available? Is it in a new
   or saturated market? What additional costs will you have
   to take on to execute the new innovation? What investments in technology, equipment, space, or people will you
   have to make, and how much will it cost?
3. Play to strengths: Read industry reports to measure your
   company's strengths and weaknesses against direct and
   indirect competitors. Consider how your business can
   do better than them. What is the secret sauce in your
   business and your people? What personal background,
   experiences, knowledge, schooling, networks can you
   leverage?
4. Alignment with passion: This is self-explanatory, but it's
   worth mentioning because you don't want to take on a
   new venture that doesn't align with the business's mission

and purpose, which is a reflection of you. Incorporating a new innovation in your business feels like being in start-up mode; it's exciting and tiring to start and ramp up, so you have to love it.

Treat this new addition to your business as if it is a small start-up. Plan for the operational, sales, marketing, and human resource needs of the growth opportunity or innovation and think about how it will affect your current operations.

FORECASTING REVENUE

Once you have estimated your start-up costs and when you need to spend that money, forecast revenue. If you are expecting to make one million dollars in revenue, be very specific about how many of each type of project, how many of each product, or how many customers of a certain type you will need to make your targeted revenue goal. The intention when doing revenue projections is to estimate the amount of revenue needed and the timing of when cash will come in to coincide with when you have to spend money on production, operations, debt and investor repayment, taxes, and your salary. If you foresee a revenue shortfall, you will need financing. So part of the planning includes researching potential sources of funds, their terms, and requirements.

IMPLEMENTATION

Once you have decided on how your operations, sales, marketing and client service or product delivery will change and put some numbers around it, it's time to implement the strategy. In *Traction*, Gino Wickman offers a way to break down your one-year revenue and profit goals into quarterly milestones that he refers to as "Rocks." They are three to seven of the most important priorities for your company to focus on and get done in ninety days to get closer to your desired revenue and profit goal. The way it works is that you set ninety-day Rocks at the beginning of each quarter, and by year end, you would have accomplished twelve to twenty-eight specific tasks that should result in achievement of your one-year revenue and profit goals.

TESTING. TRACKING. TWEAKING.

Once you put a plan into action, track your business's financial performance and tweak your strategy, cost, and revenue estimates as you go along. Leverage your strategic advisers to make this entire process smoother. Work with an outsourced CFO, financial consultant, and/or business adviser who is familiar with your type of business to help you think through your growth strategy, create financial projections, and test them assuming different scenarios.

THE PITFALLS OF NOT PLANNING

Although many business owners know it is important to have a financial plan, it is not a common practice. So it is worth mentioning some of the major pitfalls of not planning for the future.

§ Being unprepared for hyper-growth: You will max out the capacity of the current workforce and operations, which can lead to employee and customer dissatisfaction.

§ Overspending and doing what it takes to make the growth opportunity successful, which can drain your bank account.

§ Investing in an idea for growth that was not financially viable in the first place.

Geri is a serial entrepreneur, market researcher, and small business expert who speaks and writes for major publications and corporations about the trends and challenges faced by diverse founders, women owners, and funding. When she started her first business, she used all of her savings to build a product that never really gained traction with customers; so she was in the hole for that money. Investors often recommend business owners bootstrap (funding a business with money from personal savings, friends and family, and initial sales) their business early on instead of giving up equity in exchange for investor funding. Geri tried to work her way back from that situation for a long time funding her business with credit cards, and then she tried to look for lower-cost/lower interest rate alternatives. The difficulty she encountered in searching for low-cost funding led her to much of the research and articles Geri produces today, exposing challenges that women and people of color entrepreneurs face funding their businesses and accessing capital in general.

Once you have a strategy in place for the future, communicate it to your employees. Remember to tie a financial metric to each employee's role and measure of performance so they too are tied to the increased profitability of your business. This practice engenders a sense of pride and collective ownership in the success of the business. With incentivized employees and a profitable business, what is possible for us as business owners is an increase in personal wealth and financial freedom.

Now I want to take a moment to dive back into a previous thought about raising prices originally introduced in Chapter 4 (Ten Cash Commandments).

USE PRICE AS A LEVER TO INCREASE REVENUE

The two parts to the revenue equation are price and quantity. Revenue equals price times quantity (for example, $1,000 in revenue = $50 price x 200 units sold), which means that when you tweak one part of the equation, revenue is affected. To increase revenue and profits, small business owners default to ratcheting up marketing efforts in the hopes of attracting more customers and increasing the quantity of products and services sold.

Instead, strategically increase prices. It is a powerful lever to increase revenue and profits. If you just increase prices by 5 percent, look at the impact to your bottom line. Clients might not even feel the difference. I know raising prices is easier said than done. It was hard for me in the first few years of business. I was afraid to ask and risk losing customers. I was also under that false pretense that because my company is mission driven, my pricing should be accessible and affordable to as many business owners as possible. Branding myself as an outsourced CFO was a hard sell years ago before it became a popularized title. So I thought since most business owners are just accustomed to working with a CPA and bookkeeper, I'd charge what they charge. I figured small business owners would not be willing to pay my prices.

Two instances made me change my approach. A business adviser said, "You have to set up to serve." This meant I can't serve the people if I can't support my own household and personal goals. I worked on a project for six months and after it ended the client said he would have paid more for my services. That's all I needed to hear, but I still wasn't sure by how much to increase prices. I made enough to cover current expenses, personal costs, and have a bit of savings.

A business mentor suggested I think about how much money I helped clients make and save and the value I brought personally serving as a go-to sounding board for critical decision-making. I considered the complexity of the problems clients presented, the average salary of a full-time CFO working in a mid-sized business, the invaluable network of professionals I can call on to provide complementary services, and most importantly, the years of experience and knowledge I brought from Wharton, Fuqua, Wall Street, and a diversity of small nonprofit and for-profit organizations. I eventually started increasing prices by 10 percent for each subsequent client until I got resistance.

My pricing strategy was value based. You must consider many factors to determine the right price for your product or service. In fact, a whole field of marketing and finance focuses on pricing and pricing strategies. But you don't have to be an MBA or a McKinsey consulting pricing specialist to figure out the right price, follow the four Ks to unlock the right price, make more money, and increase profits: *Know your customer. Know your competitors. Know your numbers. Know your worth.* The goal is to price your products and services for profitability.

KNOW YOUR CUSTOMER

Use a customer-led approach instead of a "you"-led approach.

You-led approach:

Tanya owns a gourmet bakery and considered adding two innovations to her business: selling complementary products (a yellow cake baking mix) and services (cooking classes in the fall and winter). She went full force into figuring out what resources (staff, licenses, technology, manufacturers, etc.) she needed to make this happen and asked her marketing person to create the promotional assets and come up with a strategy to launch the products and services in six months. Tanya invested in these additional revenue streams and priced the baking mix and cooking classes according to what she thought people would pay for it as well as what competitors and local grocers charged. Tanya's baking mix didn't really take off, and the interest in cooking classes were only seasonal.

Customer-led approach:

Mike B., an artist-turned-restaurant owner from Chicago, recounted a time when he was looking for ways to increase his profit margin. Profit margin is the percent of revenue left over after paying for the cost of goods or services (supplies, materials, ingredients, labor, packaging, shipping and delivery). He reviewed the sales over time of different foods and beverages in his point-of-sale system and realized the Sparkling Roses drink was very popular. It was an alcoholic beverage made with simple ingredients and cost very little to make. It was very popular; the problem was that Mike B. and his staff weren't proud of the drink. "We resented the fact that it was on the menu because we were artists who created amazing craft cocktails. Sparkling Roses was a pedestrian drink." But when Mike B. saw how much money the beverage made, he used cheaper ingredients, increased the portion size, and increased the price.

That was one product where he was able to increase the profit margins by reducing the cost to make it, charge a premium price and drive sales because customer demand was high. Mike B. has since sold the restaurant, but in retrospect, he believes that Sparkling Roses and their historical burger nights probably kept his restaurant alive. He recalls lines crawling out the door on certain nights for those two items.

Mike B. focused on what the customer wanted and valued while Tanya offered a product and service she thought customers would want at a price she thought they would pay. By using the customer-led approach, you will be able to charge more than you thought you could, resulting in higher-than-expected profits. Bain and Company's research identified thirty elements of value or metrics on which people measure whether they will purchase something and how much they are willing to pay. These elements fall into four categories: functional, emotional, life changing, and social impact. Some elements are more inwardly focused, primarily addressing consumers' personal needs. Others are outwardly focused, helping customers interact in or navigate the external world (HBR, 2016). It took me many years in business to understand what clients valued and how to price it accordingly, and I'm still learning.

KNOW YOUR COMPETITORS

The second way to unlock the right price and make more money is to know your competitors, both direct and indirect. If you have a vegan bakery, other vegan bakeries in the area are direct competitors, but indirect competitors include local groceries that carry vegan items Whole Foods, specialty vegan caterers, and smoothie and juice bars.

Business Type	Direct Competitors	Indirect Competition
Vegan bakery	Vegan caterer, vegan eatery	Local vegan health food market,Whole Foods
Natural hair care products	Natural hair care brands in Target, home-made products	Natural hair stylist
Business coach	S.C.O.R.E and Small Business Development Center (SBDC) mentors	CPAs,CFOs, marketing specialists

Compare and contrast competitor pricing. Don't just take their pricing as the gold standard. This approach assumes the competition is correct in their pricing and knows in absolute terms what the market values are. You would miss the opportunity to raise prices due to demand for your particular product or service.

If competitor prices are not easily visible or available, do research on the following to get a sense of what they offer and what customers value about their product and service offering:

§ their strengths and weaknesses as compared to yours—identify areas where they pose a threat or reveal a market opportunity that you can also leverage.

§ their target client—is their target audience exactly like yours, or is there a niche you can carve out for your business by location, age, stage of life, etc.? If you have a vegan bakery, offer baking classes if competitors don't and your customer values that experience. If you have a natural hair care company, provide tutorials on how to use your products.

§ the features and benefits offered to the client—Apple products offer functionality and cool. Disney offers family friendly magic, wonder, and fun. Gatorade offers performance fuel and makes you look like a professional.

§ social media presence, frequency, followers, and engagement

KNOW YOUR NUMBERS

One of the greatest challenges prospective clients have is figuring out if they are charging enough. I often hear of business owners using the cost-plus pricing model, which means they consider the direct cost of creating a product or delivering a service and then add some random percentage markup or intended rate of return.

One of the pitfalls to the cost-plus pricing approach is there's little incentive to cut costs or find lower-cost alternative suppliers, vendors, and laborers because this approach inherently assumes the cost of production is fixed. Second, there is a missed opportunity to differentiate your pricing by customer type, location, or other segments to generate more profits.

For example, if you have a fitness business and use cost-plus pricing, you will miss out on the chance to generate more revenue by offering different membership levels. The last pitfall of this approach is that you're not factoring in the customer's willingness to pay a premium.

Instead of using the cost-plus approach, use the break-even approach to figure out the minimum price to charge to cover overhead (payroll, rent, utilities, travel, office expenses) and variable costs of producing a good or service.

A bakery selling cheesecake has the following costs

- § Cost of ingredients: $8 per cheesecake
- § Cost of direct labor: $12 per cheesecake
- § Packaging supplies: $3 per cheesecake
- § Total fixed costs: $225,000

For 15,000 cheesecakes, the break-even price = ($225,000 divided by 15,000 cheesecakes) + $23 = $38

For 10,000 cheesecakes, the break-even price = ($225,000/10,000) + $23 = $45.50

For 18,000 cheesecakes, the break-even price = ($225,000/18,000) + $23 = $35.50

Thirty-eight dollars, $45.50, and $35.50 are the lowest prices this baker should charge customers if they plan to sell that number of cheesecakes in a given year. Any price charged above the break-even price will result in profit, but you have to also consider a price commensurate with where competitors are priced or what clients are willing to pay. So the bigger the difference between what you charge and the break-even price, the higher the potential profits.

An IT services company providing remote IT-managed services for doctor's private practice chains has the following costs.

§ Software and cyber security licensing costs per computer/printer serviced: $12
§ Average labor costs per computer serviced: $65
§ Total annual fixed costs: $250,000

To service 2,400 computers and printers, the break-even price = ($250,000 divided by 2,400 computers) + $77 direct costs = break-even prices of about $181 per computer serviced. These calculations become a bit more complicated when you factor in multiple products and services. But the point remains the same: pricing can really impact profitability if you control operating expenses and direct costs.

KNOW YOUR WORTH

Once you have learned what your customer values, gathered intel on competitor's pricing and strategies, calculated the break-even price, and determined the optimal price for your products and services, make the ask.

If you have tremendous experience, you've been in the industry/function for a long time, and you add value to customers and clients, you can charge a slight premium. But if you are new to the industry and haven't built much brand awareness or brand loyalty, start off at the lower end of the market range and then gradually increase to and above market rate.

Sometimes knowing your worth means knowing when to say "no." When you started your businesses, gaining as many clients and revenue as possible was important for survival but once business has been stabilized, it is quite okay to be a bit more selective about clients that don't fit the target profile. Redirect them to peers in your industry that are a better fit. That simple act of kindness may turn into a referral from the same person to a more appropriate client.

Entrepreneurship gave Ruoyun the opportunity to dance with her pricing, albeit awkwardly at first. It took her six years and two businesses to feel comfortable charging what her time and knowledge are actually worth. She is currently an outsourced chief marketing officer and speaker specializing in humanizing digital marketing. She is a serial entrepreneur, formerly managing the branch of a vector marketing company and running her own digital marketing agency.

Ruoyun struggled with increasing the prices of her digital marketing agency services, even though the business did not generate enough revenue to support payroll, rent, and general operations. Ruoyun started to make different choices after following and listening to motivational speaker and pricing consultant, Casey Brown in her signature TED Talk, "Know Your Worth, And Then Ask For It!" Casey said, "No one will ever pay you what you're worth. They will only pay you what they think you're worth and you control what they're thinking!" In order to earn what you are worth and realize your full earning potential, Casey suggests defining your value *and* communicating your value. This is a tough one for many women entrepreneurs, but Casey provides a formula for success.

To define your value, ask yourself, *What problems do I solve for clients? What is my unique skill set that makes me better qualified to serve my clients? What do I do that no one else does?*

To communicate your value, embrace your natural style, find your own voice, and focus on adding value to the client.

Ruoyun also relayed the story of a famous author who was uncomfortable asking for a higher rate for speaking engagements. The author had a limiting belief that speakers who charged a lot of money must be greedy or inauthentic. But after years of speaking the author realized that by charging more, let's say $20,000 instead of $10,000 for a speaking engagement, it did not make her a "sell-out." Instead by charging more per event, the author needed fewer events to make her revenue goal, her schedule freed up and she had more bandwidth to do pro bono work for the non-profits she cared about.

Inspired by this story, Ruoyun increased prices for the chief marketing officer projects she currently takes on. As a result, she has more time to focus on creating accessible content for all marketers to learn how to humanize the way they do marketing. I realized that in reality I can at most mentally have bandwidth to impact about fifteen clients per year, but with the accessible content via YouTube, I can inspire hundreds more.

Updating your pricing is not a "one and done" exercise. It's not something you set and forget. Review your pricing every couple years to account for inflation, market changes, the cost of growth, and the value of your company's experience and equity. You will eventually hit a price ceiling, but it's healthy to always assess how you're pitching your value and assessing if you need to increase your pricing. After all, if you were an employee, you would want a raise every year or two, wouldn't you?

A FINAL WORD

By following the five critical actions to strengthen your business's financial core—Actively manage cash flow, Be performance driven, Build business credit, Reduce risk, Plan for the future—you'll grow and scale a financially healthy business. That means you can afford to hire the people you need, reward the talent already in-house, pay yourself what you need, and ultimately make the impact you want in your families and communities. Isn't that what it's all about? Achieving goals and the gold.

SECTION 3

SOAR

CHAPTER 7

Don't Freestyle Your Financials

In the Alvin Ailey American Dance Theatre's signature work, Revelation, a duet is performed to the spiritual song, "Fix Me Jesus." Toward the end of the duet the woman executes a beautiful layout, which is a jazz and ballet dance move that requires one leg to be extended with foot pointed toward the sky while the other standing leg is straight all while she arches backward until her back is parallel to the ground. To execute this move she is supported by her partner who provides enough resistance and counterbalance to prevent her from falling backward. She is the lead dancer in this piece, but I would dare say that her ability to be excellent in that moment was supported by having the right partner whom she trusts.

TRUST BUT VERIFY

It is metaphorically the same for business owners in that to reach peak performance it takes the support and trust of your financial dance partners—CPAs, bookkeepers, CFOs, bankers, and others. According to everyone I interviewed, trust played a huge part in their decision to hire someone to manage the finances of their business. I get it. This is the most vulnerable part of your business, and I know many feel that how they manage their business affairs is a reflection on themselves and their capabilities personally. So if the financials look a mess, people judge themselves personally and don't want others to know they are a mess. The fear of judgment and selecting someone who turns out to be nefarious is real for so many. That's why most of our clients come by referral or after a couple of conversations.

There are a few other criteria on which to assess any of the accounting or financial professionals you hire. Check out their credentials and speak with references. One client did a simple background check on me and my company. Confirm the person hired does the kind of work that you need. For example, don't assume all CFOs create projections or that all CPAs do tax reporting. By doing due diligence on the trusted advisers you hire, you'll avoid a world of headache. Finally, ask for the professional's policy around frequency of meetings and communication via phone, text, or email so you know how accessible they will be to you.

MAKE THE INVESTMENT

At every stage of growth, you need advisers with specific levels of expertise. This is certainly true for the accounting and financial aspects of the business. Your CPA should not do everything related to the numbers. In fact, at a certain stage (e.g., businesses with greater than twenty employees, complex operations, greater than $500,000 in revenue, lots of transactions) no single person should be managing all the financial related tasks of a business. There should be some checks and balances in place to reduce the risk of errors, theft, and fraud. Remember Anthony C. from Chapter 5? He had a very complex ten-plus-million-dollar business with hundreds of employees and had one bookkeeper running everything. That was a recipe for disaster.

In the same way you prioritize sales, marketing, and hiring, invest in a team of financial dance partners with the skills to improve the profitability, cash flow, and overall health of their business. Don't wait until times of crisis (e.g., needing access to capital) or necessity (e.g., tax reporting time). Don't penny pinch around this area of your business either by trying to do things yourself or hiring someone with little technical knowledge. The cost of cleaning up accounting errors, financial mistakes, and tax compliance issues far outweighs the cost to hire capable people to manage the numbers and accounting systems correctly in the first place. It took Anthony C. about two years and six figures to fix his problem with the IRS. If a financial person or a team saves your business money, drives client payments in the door, or helps you tweak things to generate more revenue, profits, and cash flow, make the investment.

In my experience business owners rarely know how much to budget for an accounting or financial professional whether full-time or part-time. There are so many competing messages and offerings.

1. One approach would be to look at the average full-time salaries of each of these roles on Indeed, LinkedIn, or Glassdoor and base your budget on a percentage of that salary.
2. Another approach would be to poll fellow business owners who have hired accounting and finance people in the past. Ask them what they paid.
3. The third approach requires thinking of your financial advisers not as expenses (people you spend money on) but instead as assets (people you value that will add value to your company). Try this. Quantify in dollars how much you would pay (if money was not a deterrent) to have your greatest financial challenge solved. Let's say you are willing to pay $100,000 in a year for the solution to your greatest financial challenge and you actually spend $62,000 on a CPA, outsourced bookkeeping service and an outsourced CFO in a year, then I say you are winning. You got a whole team at an equivalent to one employee's salary.

Start with a nominal investment and go from there.

WHO TO HIRE?

Meagan B. and her partner relied on their CPA and lawyer for business advice. In the early years, they were pretty out of touch with their bakery's profitability and where it stood financially overall other than making sure enough money was in the bank to pay employees and cover rent and baking ingredients. They tried to learn accounting and financial concepts on their own by taking classes at a community college,

Google University, and DIY University (both fictional universities). They even took on and shared bookkeeping tasks. Meagan B. said it felt daunting and overwhelming yet exciting to take on these responsibilities because it made her feel a sense of ownership over the business. But she had no time to deal with employee issues and grow sales post-pandemic.

By the time I met Meagan B., she was ready to add to her financial team, but she, like many business owners, had no idea whether to hire a bookkeeper, controller, or CFO. Who you hire and how much you invest in them depends on several factors including your stage of business, the complexity of your business, the level of experience and expertise of the financial professional and, how long you need the services. The bottom line is to start with a CPA and as you scale, add to your accounting and financial department so you have the right expertise and guidance at the right time.

Hire financial advisors based on your growth stage

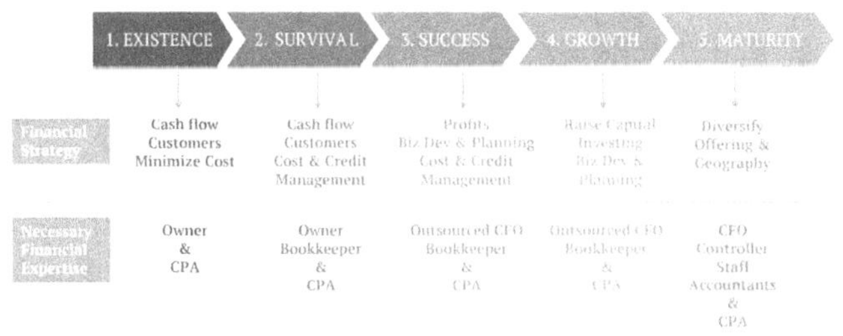

The five stages of small business growth are start-up, survival, sustainability, growth, maturity (Churchill and Lewis, 1983).

EXISTENCE

At the existence stage the financial focus is on generating revenue (through revenue generation, investors, friends and family, etc.) and managing cash flow to cover start-up costs.

Every business owner should hire a Certified Public Accountant (CPA) to:

- § advise on the appropriate business structure and provide general business advice;
- § report taxes to federal, state, and local agencies;
- § suggest the best tax strategy given their business and personal circumstances; and
- § some CPAs also offer payroll administration, sales tax payments, and bookkeeping services at an additional fee to their tax advisory services.

All CPAs are accountants, but *NOT all accountants are CPAs*. CPAs are accountants who have met state licensing requirements and passed a CPA exam. All CPAs don't do tax reporting and planning, so inquire before hiring. They also specialize in audits, forensic accounting, financial reviews, or other industry-specific matters.

The CPA's added value: CPAs and enrolled agents can represent their clients in front of the IRS on any matters including audits, payment/collection issues, and appeals.

SURVIVAL

A business in this stage has established its place in the world with a flow of customers, a more clearly defined product or service offering and value proposition. Many business owners at this stage realize they have not been handling their numbers, credit, nor their financial operations properly. They then start seeking help to clean up their books, access capital, and handle a full suite of accounting tasks.

The solution is to add a bookkeeper to your financial team to:

§ record financial transactions, reconcile accounts, and prepare financial statements.
§ handle invoicing and collections.
§ manage vendor and contractor payments.
§ handle some payroll and HR functions.
§ work with tax preparers, assisting with tax compliance, reporting, and sales tax payments.

IMPORTANT: Make sure the bookkeeper has prior experience in accounting, not just experience using accounting software.

Although you might start out using the bookkeepers within your CPA's firm, there are compelling reasons to maintain a separation between church and state. A colleague managing a unisex hair salon asked me to give an independent assessment of the salon's financial position. Unfortunately, he didn't have ready access to his books and had to rely on his CPA to know whether the company was profitable or solvent. After two months, we finally received a copy of their financial statements and not only was it not up to date, but it revealed that my colleagues' business had been operating at a loss for a few months.

Here's three reasons to keep your bookkeeper in-house and your CPA external.

1. As your business grows, you will want someone dedicated to your business who is not serving hundreds of people at a CPA firm and who has intimate knowledge of your finances in case you need to make a quick decision like cut a last-minute check, respond to a tax notice, provide bankers financial reports, or strategically cut costs.
2. It's good to have two sets of eyes on your numbers. The bookkeeper will know the ins and outs of your business, but the CPA will verify that the books are in compliance with accounting rules. If transactions aren't categorized properly, financial statements will be unreliable and you won't be able to make critical business decisions.
3. If bookkeeping is kept in-house, you will have better control over your financials and ready access to information for decision-making. But, if it is housed by the CPA, your books may not receive attention until tax time.

The bookkeeper's added value: The more savvy, experienced bookkeepers know how to optimize accounting platforms and other financial technology to manage their tasks more efficiently thus, saving them time and you money.

SUCCESS AND GROWTH

"The decision facing owners at this stage is whether to exploit the company's accomplishments and expand or keep the company stable and profitable, providing a base for alternative owner activities" (Churchill and Lewis, 1983). At this point the business is generating profits, there are a decent amount of cash reserves, and the business has enough assets to cover its liabilities (what is owed to vendors and lenders). The financial strategy at these stages is focused on maintaining the health (profitability, cash flow strength, and solvency) of the business in the midst of growth or scale and strategic planning for the future.

Business owners at this stage have even less time to oversee the numbers, back-office operations, and external parties. They need an executive leader, a financial choreographer of sorts, with a high level of technical skill to direct all financial activity, a creative imagination to forecast the future, and the stamina to drive the company to peak performance. This is when you add an outsourced chief financial officer (CFO) to your accounting/financial team. If your business generates less than fifteen million dollars in revenue, you probably don't need a full-time CFO; a fractional (outsourced, virtual) one would suffice.

An outsourced CFO's responsibilities are customized to our clients' needs and challenges, but they can generally handle the following:

- § cash flow and expense management
- § access to debt and equity capital
- § budgets and forecasts
- § measuring and monitoring financial health
- § making investment decisions
- § bookkeeping oversight and risk management

If you are wondering whether you need an outsourced CFO at the success and growth business stages, you can't afford *not* to have one! This is particularly true for business owners generating $500,000 or more in revenue, supporting employees and contractors, and inquiring about complex issues like:

§ pricing
§ the financial impact of adding new products and services or completely pivoting the business
§ how to control cash burn and extend your runway in times of crisis
§ what assumptions and factors to include in future projections
§ whether to fund the business through debt or equity and how to manage that process
§ how to increase the value of a business
§ preparing for an exit, merger, or acquisition

If any of these scenarios resonated with you, hire an outsourced CFO experienced in your company's unique circumstances; don't expect a CPA or bookkeeper to have these answers. That is not usually part of their expertise. Every member of your financial team has their skillset and purpose.

Arijit, owner of an artificial intelligence company, said, "Nobody ever *needs* a CFO." But he followed this thought with, "If the business gets more and more complicated, bringing in a good CFO, makes your life so much easier and provides good controls. They end up being a trusted adviser who keeps you from looking at life through rose colored glasses... The job of your CFO is to control and manage the imagination and natural optimism of the entrepreneur...What makes for a really good CFO is sometimes a lack of imagination because the CFO has to be very, very structured; they have to be saying, 'I don't care what your optimism is telling you; I'm gonna look at the numbers'."

Ruoyun, the marketing expert, recommends her peers work with outsourced CFOs who are not only strategic but who also will implement recommendations and educate you about the numbers, along the way. She said, "I was very lucky that the universe, allowed me to connect with my CFO who trained me and guided me and gave me tough love. She is not like the traditional fractional CFO who just gives you reports; she teaches you how to read your books and understand your numbers."

WHAT IS THE DIFFERENCE BETWEEN WHAT YOU DO AND WHAT A CONTROLLER DOES?

I get this question all the time. Many people use the terms controller and CFO interchangeably, but each role is different. Controllers are high-level accountants who maintain quality control over the numbers. They are sticklers for following generally accepted accounting principles and making sure strong controls, policies, and processes are in place. Controllers are most valuable to construction, manufacturing, e-commerce, and hyper-growth start-up companies where the accounting is more complex and GAAP-based accounting is necessary.

While a controller is great at documenting the past and relying on historical information, they are not as strong at forecasting the future and looking at the financial impact of different scenarios. This is where a CFO thrives. A CFO has a strong enough accounting background to oversee a small business's financial department and has the creative mind to do future planning as well. In a large organization, a CFO is more senior to a controller, but in a small business, hire one or the other depending on your business's needs and unique issues.

MATURITY

At this phase of the business's journey, the primary financial focus is optimizing the value of the business. It is at this point small business owners make a major decision to grow the business by expanding into other markets, build a new technology to scale operations, or exit completely. No matter what direction you take at this stage, the financial operations tend to be so complicated that you need a full financial team led by a full-time CFO.

The financial team should include a bookkeeper or junior accountant, a senior accountant and/or controller, and other accounting or financial professionals (i.e., accounts payable clerk, accounts receivable clerk, financial analyst) depending on your business needs.

ADDING OTHERS TO THE MIX

Sometimes you need a little extra help beyond the services a CPA, bookkeeper, and CFO provide. A client worked with one hundred subcontractors and suppliers at any given time. So in addition to a CPA and bookkeeper, he hired an accounts payable clerk to manage vendor and 1099's bills, payments, complaints, and inquiries. Another client hired an HR specialist and recruiter in-house to manage the complaints, questions, and turnover of his workforce of 350 union and non-union employees. If you have ten or more employees, you need more than just a payroll service provider. You need HR support; start with a part-time person or outsourced service.

Danielle is a former marketing manager who grew a multi-million-dollar business teaching people to turn their passion/expertise into online courses. The money habits that she brought into her business were ones of achievement and financial independence, which she learned from her mother. Danielle's dad was the bookkeeper and budgeter in the household, but she did not have a natural inclination toward math, accounting, and financial matters. She first learned about building forecasts from a former boss at a start-up. By the time Danielle started her business, she had enough savvy to build a simple model for her sales and revenue goals in a spreadsheet. She said, "My spreadsheet and I were best friends."

When her business grew, Danielle hired a bookkeeper who provided her a dashboard of the most critical performance metrics for her to review monthly. Then she added a CFO to oversee the bookkeeping and help her manage team costs, overall profitability, and cash flow. The CPA guided Danielle's domestic and international tax strategy. After a few years, Danielle launched other businesses, grew to eight figures, and owned a portfolio of businesses. She needed specialty advice, so she hired an executive business consultant with experience scaling multi-million-dollar businesses.

The consultant taught her many things including how to think about investing in other opportunities using capital from the main business; how investing in other businesses would impact the holding company's balance sheet; and how to optimize margins in spite of a growing team. Danielle credits her financial dance partners with helping her understand the relationship between her numbers and her dream life so she can execute smoothly.

THE SUPPORTING CAST

Small business owners learned so many lessons in the 2020 recession and pandemic. One that stands out is the importance of having a relationship with bankers, alternative lenders, and other gatekeepers of capital. If you maintain a strong relationship with lenders and investors before you actually need to ask for money, you'll stand a better chance at getting funded.

When the SBA announced the Paycheck Protection Program (PPP) in April 2020, I called my business banker before the bank even set up a site to accept applications. I assumed the money would run out early so I wanted to be prepared and help my clients prepare their application package as well. When my bank started accepting applications, my banker notified me on the first day, and my applications and those of our clients were ready to go also.

You stand a better chance of accessing capital when the keepers of cash know you. Research which lending institutions are the best fit for your business needs. Large traditional banks are often the default source for lending, but a small regional bank or credit union may be more appropriate. They tend to have more flexibility in who they can lend to and the type of deal structures they can create. Community development financial institutions (CDFIs) are great alternative lenders often providing better rates and terms. Be advised their loan process tends to be longer and more involved than that of traditional banks. Often traditional banks and credit unions partner with CDFIs to provide businesses funding. SBA lenders may be the best option for start-up businesses or those established businesses that have sufficient cash flow but lack a full two to three years of financials, necessary collateral, or a good credit history.

Select two or three lenders to build relationships with by staying in communication ever so often (maybe quarterly) and providing updates on how the business is growing and performing. Follow up with any information lenders request. Be upfront with all your financial information, and if there are issues, be prepared to explain how you're resolving them. Have the lender visit your office, production plant, or store so they know how you run things. Refer a fellow entrepreneur if they are also seeking capital or guidance. All these little steps put you at the front of the service line when the time comes.

Equity investors also value relationship building. In an *Inc* article, Dave Bailey, a serial entrepreneur and venture partner, said, "As an investor, I learned that there are really only two reasons to invest in a start-up. The first is demonstrable traction...the second reason is because I've known the founders for a long time, I trust them, and they occupy the position of 'terrifyingly talented' in my head." He suggests start-up founders approach this process like a marketer but use good judgment.

§ Build a target list of investors or associates at seed and VC funds.
§ Find out the investors' individual needs and how you can help them.
§ Get in touch—craft a short, pointed, irresistible email that makes them say yes to you.
§ Follow up regularly with short, relevant, and them-focused messages.
§ Be patient.

THE UNSUNG DANCE PARTNERS

When interviewing business owners for this book, many of them had CPAs. But before they invested in a bookkeeper, controller, or any other accounting/finance professional, they relied on business partners, spouses, and advisers at small business centers to help them manage the numbers. Malika J. and Erin had their husbands and in-laws help them navigate business issues and provide invaluable moral support. As an entrepreneur, having a partner with a steady paycheck and health insurance can be a saving grace. Luam K. talked about having a money team—experts and non-experts—who speak to you about money freely, share a new money-saving app they're using, or refer you to a professional who can help solve your money problem. "The way that wealthy people stay wealthy is that they talk about their money freely and all the time. They love sharing tips, secrets, and ideas."

Michael B. found himself in a cash crunch and tight debt situation at one point in his ten years in business. He met with a small business development center (SBDC) mentor to help him unravel the situation. He recalls "her suggestions being too big at the time though she gave sound advice to invest more in his business so he could make more." But at a critical moment, Michael B. needed help to settle some debt obligations and limit the negative implications to his credit profile. This is when his lawyer had to step in. When the going gets tough, get the right lawyer involved.

When Joe started his marketing agency, he defaulted all the financial tasks to his first business partner, but he later found out that partner was not good with credit management. Before taking on his next partner, Joe made sure the person had good credit. He said, "I wanted to see how they spent money. I wanted to see how they made money. I wanted to see how they lived their life. I wanted to see how much money they had and whether or not they were doing the work for the money or because they were into the work." Besides this new partner, Joe also relies on peers in his business masterminds whose advice he trusts because they have come to know his business more intimately over the years. Vistage, Entrepreneur's Organization, Young Jewish Professionals, INC500 Business Owners Council, and other similar networks provide mastermind circles led by executive coaches and consultants who can complement the advice of accounting and financial experts.

In order to dance with your numbers, get dance partners and financial choreographers that are trustworthy, make your job easier and help you avoid pitfalls. A bookkeeper will organize the financial records and handle the day-to-day back-office operations while your controller and outsourced CFO can provide insights from your data and help you increase the financial health of the business. Depend on your financial team to counterbalance your optimism and help you think strategically about how to grow and scale your business in the future.

Just as professional athletes and performers need different coaches (strength coach, physical therapist, technical specialist, vocal coach, assistant choreographers, artistic directors) to keep them at peak performance, you will also need a team of specialists including bankers, lenders, business mentors, and even friends and family to help you achieve the financial goals for your business and ultimately your life. Whether your money team includes two or ten people, as you grow through each business stage, be sure to invest in your finance department.

Getting to Peak Performance

When I was hired as an ensemble dancer in the Tony award-winning Broadway musical *Fela!*, we prepared for two months in studio and continued perfecting the flow of the production during the tour. I learned my track (all the places I needed to be on the stage and the pathways to get there), the songs, dance numbers, and acting numbers, so that the music and dance moves were mostly in my body by the time that we hit the first theater. But it took the entire length of the tour for me to really understand and truly embody the soul and the life of my role, that show, and the lives it represented. That's because no matter how well we performed, how much we sounded like a collective voice or marched as one unit on and off the stage, there was always another lesson or note for improvement meant to up our level of performance on stage.

It was a very emotionally and physically demanding show and I remember what it took for me to be at peak performance for over one hundred shows across over fifteen cities. Even though I was physically strong, I had to follow a restorative mind/body practice, balance between time spent with the company and taking personal time to explore cities, stay connected to my people back home who rejuvenated me, and keep perfecting challenging moves.

My experience as a business owner has been similar. I continuously work on improving myself, try to find the right teammates and partners, switch up sales and marketing tactics, and look for new approaches to my work to ensure the business is profitable, my family's future is secure, and women entrepreneurs are empowered. Getting to peak financial performance in business requires a different mindset, expanded knowledge and continuous improvement through conventional and non-conventional ways. Small business center mentor Carolyn K. said, "What [small business owners] don't understand is that to continue growing their business to peak performance, it takes a different mindset than how you thought when you started the business." In this chapter, I touch on actions business owners have taken beyond strengthening their financial core to reach their business and personal goals.

LEVEL UP YOUR KNOWLEDGE

To get to peak performance, you have to strike a balance between growing sales and making sure you have enough profit or, more importantly, cash flow to keep the business going.

Libby R. is a registered dietitian. She teaches other independent dietitians to build a sustainable, profitable practice from soup to nuts. Coming from a single-parent home, the most important thing Libby R. learned about money was that she needed to be financially independent so she could take care of herself and make her own life decisions. The money lessons her mom taught her as a youngster became the biggest influence in who she is as a person and as a business owner. Her money behavior and mindset can best be described as that of a go-getter, achiever, and hustler. She began working since the age of eleven and built a profitable personal training business at nineteen through strong sales and marketing ability. She said, "Making money is my gift."

She leveraged her killer sales skills to quickly grow her business to a million dollars in revenue. When Libby R. started her business, she focused on three key things: building a differentiated brand, tweaking her services to her target customer's needs, and sales growth. She kept financial planning very simple—setting revenue and sales goals and periodically tracking progress against those goals. The only performance metrics she used to measure business health were sales and marketing metrics: leads, qualified leads, prospects, calls booked, deals closed, and conversion ratios. But she wasn't paying attention to expenses, profits, or cash burn to see if revenue was enough to keep the lights on.

The trigger moment that broadened Libby's knowledge of key performance metrics was when she had to calculate other non-sales data points as a homework assigned by her accelerator program. She learned then that it's not all about sales and marketing, she had to know numbers like customer satisfaction, employee billable versus non-billable hours, and employee retention rate. After that trigger moment, Libby's mindset and behaviors shifted. Her focus "[became] figuring out how to best allocate money to grow the business and strategizing on the best ways to scale." First on her priority list was hiring the right team to support the infrastructure of her company. The important thing to measure in this case was the percent of headcount filled.

While sales and marketing are critical to drive revenue and profits, Libby R. admits she was short sighted in measuring success on just two areas of the business. That blind spot could have cost Libby R. her business, but thankfully she is still doing well and is onto the next phase, scale and maturity.

COMMUNITY AND CULTURE

I give each performance all I have and leave my heart on the stage, but I have delivered my best performances when friends and family are in the audience cheering me on. It's amazing what a strong sense of community can do. I stayed resilient during the 2020 recession and pandemic by relying on business and personal communities for positive energy, advice, information, and money-making opportunities. Team cultures were also strengthened during that time as CEOs did the best they could to hold on to their employees and in a show of camaraderie, jumped in to work alongside their people. The result was increased employee loyalty, increased employee productivity, and ultimately, increased business and profits for the company.

When the COVID-19 pandemic hit and all the data Arijit's company relied on became invalid, Arijit decided to pour more money into the business to keep his entire staff. He and his leadership team made a decision very early on that for six months they were not going to let go of anyone, and Arijit deferred his own salary. He said, "I fundamentally believe that the employees are part of the family that we have in the company, and [the 2020 pandemic] was not their fault. So, how could they be penalized?" It all worked out because during that time, the employees became even more productive and creative and devised new revenue-generating opportunities for the business, which made Arijit's company even more money. One of Arijit's heuristics is that he tries to hire the best people he possibly can even if he has to pay a high salary because he knows the employee's output is going to probably be ten times the investment he made. That way of thinking definitely paid off in this scenario.

Focusing on community and culture make huge impact in a company. It's what keeps certain companies on the Fortune 100 "Best Places to Work" list. The 2020 pandemic reinforced Michael B.'s belief that community is key to the viability and strength of a business. During our conversation he recounted how involved his Chicago restaurant was in supporting Black Lives Matter and the trans community's local initiatives and events. He said, "Chicago's all about the neighborhood...when we started to get involved with the community and give back that's when things really took off for us, and we were really doing well, morale wise." Michael B. became Mr. Community Leader a few years before the third wave of the pandemic came in the summer of 2020.

The neighborhood association where Michael B.'s restaurant was located hosted a big midsummer festival to welcome tourists to the city of Chicago. For years, the organizers put porta potties in front of Michael B.'s restaurant affecting his ability to use the outdoor patio for customer service. One year he decided to get on the planning committee and asked the board at the Chamber of Commerce to have a booth near his restaurant. He recounted, "My presence on the street, directing people's attention to our restaurant, and giving out food to people and being a part of the community just made us present and put us on the stage."

Every year thereafter, Michael B. got more involved with the festival, joined the board, and started making decisions about how the festival happened. Needless to say, no more porta potties were in front of his restaurant after that. "It was really eye-opening to see how businesses and community were intertwined, and how important that actually was for a business, a small business, to stay connected to the community. And so, I got more and more involved, and that also increased our business and increased our presence and our brand more positively."

HIRE THE RIGHT PEOPLE

You can't have great community and culture without quality people. Danielle, the online course expert introduced in Chapter 7, had a similar story to Libby R.'s story. Danielle sharpened her sales and marketing skills at her first few jobs. She worked in sales at a corporation and at a start-up company, Danielle learned how to make revenue repeatable and scalable. So, when she launched her business, driving sales was her primary focus. She set a target ad spend, a monthly revenue target, and figured out how many customers she needed at a set price point to meet that goal. Her strategy led her to build a seven-figure business in a few years.

As the business grew, Danielle realized she needed to invest a lot of her income into systems and people not just sales and marketing. She used to handle most everything herself until one day she returned home from a vacation to over three hundred emails and another few hundred customer inquiries on her site. She knew her first hire needed to be a customer support person. Over the years, Danielle's mindset around investing in people completely changed. She said, "The key is to hire someone who can give you more peace of mind; hire that person first. Hire the person who is going to give you a holistic return on investment. Think of a hire the same way you would an investment in new technology. If the person is going to give a ten-times return in their role, I don't care how expensive they are."

If Danielle could speak to herself in year one of business, the first thing she would have done was hire an executive assistant, who had the spiritual "groundedness," savvy, and experience to not just manage her calendar but also to serve as her thought partner in business. Danielle attributes some of her personal success and growth to hiring good people, having mentors in her corner, and reading self-improvement books as part of her daily practice. She referred to her health coaches, spiritual adviser, business mentor, and a few others whom she kept in close proximity as her visionaries. They keep her performing at her best as a CEO and human being. She said, "They get me in closer proximity to myself."

GET YOUR MIND RIGHT

The second thing Danielle would have done her first year in business was to establish a morning ritual to get her energized in her day. Hal Elrod, author of the popular productivity book *Miracle Morning*, claims that the six practices in the Miracle Morning routine, called SAVERS, are "guaranteed to save you from a life of unfulfilled potential." Danielle believes wholeheartedly in the importance of having a morning routine, which includes prayer or meditation, exercise, and other health habits; it is a part of the signature course that helped her achieve much success.

Danielle was not the only business owner I interviewed who focused on personal improvement or some sort of restorative practice to fortify their mind, improve their physical health, and ground their spirit. In fact, Joe A., the LinkedIn expert and marketing agency owner, is always working on mindset. He said, "Today my mindset is so strong because I dedicated time and money to developing that muscle after multiple challenges occurred within a five-year time frame from divorcing a business partner, to losing a key employee, to losing about over 70 percent of recurring revenue in one business and going through other personal trials."

With the highs and lows of entrepreneurship, it is inevitable that at some point all business owners have to sharpen their mind especially when they are pushed out of their comfort zone. That place of discomfort for many is dealing with the financial matters of their business and personal life. Joe thought numbers were scary in the early years of his business, but after ten years, he now has the know-how to make critical decisions for his business.

ALIGN WITH YOUR WHY

One of the ways that Ruoyun believes business owners can achieve peak performance and freely dance with their numbers, is to continuously align with *why* they are in business. Being resolute in what purpose your business fulfills for you requires mindfulness and intentionality. Ruoyun said, "The reason why the feeling of being a complete failure is so amplified when business owners make a bad financial decision, is not because they failed, but because the decision they chose wasn't aligned 100 percent to what they believed in. So not only does the feeling of rejection exist, it goes on steroids because they resent themselves for wasting time and money on something they didn't fully stand behind."

Her favorite quote by Bruce Lee gives a visual depiction of her point.

"Notice that the stiffest tree is most easily cracked, while the bamboo or willow survives by bending with the wind."

Bamboo and willows have very strong and deep roots that support the tree no matter how inclement the weather. Ruoyun's point is to be like a bamboo, rooted, in your why such that no matter if you are launching a new product/

service, firing an employee, hiring a new CPA, or dealing with IRS issues, you would not get stressed or overwhelmed. In the end everything will be okay; you will not die. By aligning to your *why*, you will be willing to take risks that push you outside your comfort zone. The conversation with Ruoyun was so interesting because one of my mottos in life is to know my why for doing something and when my why is no longer being fulfilled, it is time to move on. Sometimes your why can shift. During the 2020 pandemic, many clients' goals shifted from wanting to grow and scale to wanting to set the business up for exit.

FROM PEAK PERFORMANCE TO GRAND EXIT

Jennie, the organic ice cream company owner mentioned earlier is seriously preparing herself for exit. She jokingly said, "I serve the 10 percent EBITDA gods." What she means is that she is doing all she can to maintain a margin that is relatively high for her industry so her business is attractive to potential buyers. EBITDA stands for earnings (profit) before interest, taxes, and depreciation. It is one of the numbers used to measure the profitability of the business. The 10 percent margin she is striving for is calculated by dividing EBITDA by total revenue in a given period.

Jennie was not always this vigilant over her numbers. Jennie was an actress prior to starting her business and professes that she knew nothing about starting a business. In fact, when she started her business, her dad gifted her an accounting class, but she did not take it. In retrospect, it is the first thing Jennie said she should have done as a new business owner.

She loved math and was not taught about money basics in childhood, so Jennie had no fundamental knowledge of how to manage her business finances. She learned by force. Her partner who initially handled the financials left the business and then Jennie had a few bad situations with bookkeepers and self-proclaimed CFOs that caused more of a mess than they were worth. So Jennie decided to take it on herself committing time to analyze her numbers on a regular basis. With some training sessions from a bookkeeper friend, the help of an employee, and sheer will, she learned about all the inputs that drove her business performance and focused on improving every data point, especially her products costs.

I would not recommend any business owner do their own bookkeeping at the growth and mature stages, which is where Jennie is in her business now. But I do applaud her for understanding the performance drivers of her business. As I mentioned earlier in the book, have five to ten performance metrics that you keep a keen eye on because those are probably the same metrics you will want to optimize (especially EBITDA, cash burn, and the liabilities to assets ratio) if you want to eventually sell your business.

After years of shooting for peak performance, business owners can only hope to sell their business and receive a payout that is commensurate with the value they have created in the business. If you are planning to exit, give yourself a few years to plan and in the meantime, work with your executive team—business adviser, COO, and CFO—to improving the business's overall value while lowering its perceived risk by:

§ demonstrating consistently growing revenue and profits over the next few years;

§ projecting at least five years of strong positive cash flow;

§ reducing the business's dependence on the owner;

§ improving the business's market share, depth of management, knowledge and skillset of the workforce and operational processes; and

§ continuing to build on your most valuable assets (e.g., a technology, product line, intellectual property, client contracts). Note: tech product-based businesses tend to command a higher valuation than many service-based business.

An exit can take many forms besides selling it in the open market. You can exit through a merger, sale of owner's stake to a partner or investor, a transition of ownership to a family member or employees, an initial public offering, or a liquidation of assets (leading to a complete closure of the business). No matter the path to exit, you will need to get an appraisal of the value of your business.

The SBA suggests using these common valuation methods to value your business and seek resources for business valuation appraises from the Appraisal Foundation:

1. Income approach: looks at projected revenue and accounts for potential risks.
2. Market approach: compares your business to other similar businesses that have recently sold.
3. Assets approach: subtracts total business liabilities from the total value of all assets.

You will need the expertise of a few different specialists (e.g., a business banker, valuation specialist, forensic CPA, attorneys specializing in the type of exit, etc.) beyond your accounting and financial team to help you through the exit process. But one of the key internal employees involved in every aspect of an exit is the chief financial officer. Evan Janovic, former owner of the largest independent paint dealer in New York, Janovic Plaza Inc, spoke at an entrepreneur's roundtable I attended years ago. Mr. Janovic recounted how critical of a role his internal CFO played during that sale. His family-owned small business grew organically over 110 years through strategic acquisitions and a focus on customer satisfaction. In 1999, Benjamin Moore Paints acquired Janovic Plaza Inc. The buyer's corporate auditors had to work with Janovic Plaza Inc's full-time CFO to get the deal done. The CFO knew the business's numbers and operations well and had to help familiarize the corporate folks with the accounting and financial inner workings of a small business so they could assess the true value of the business and offer a fair price.

Now, you not only have financial strategies to improve your bottom line but also more tactical options to build a business that you're proud of. With the right talent, culture, community of neighbors, mentors, colleagues, and personal development mechanisms, you and your business will soar to new levels.

....

The Final Step

Congratulations on completing the six steps to dancing with your numbers. You are well on your way to becoming the chief financial choreographer of your business and your life! I hope that this book has given you the information to stand firmly in this role instead of feeling any sort of impostor syndrome. I truly believe that the reason business owners want to increase revenue, boost profits, and have a better command of their numbers is because they want to control their destiny, be financially free and choreograph the lives they want. For the hundreds of established business owners I have spoken to, their drive to succeed all boils down to the fact that they want to elevate their impact by contributing more meaningfully to their household, build a legacy for their children, retire comfortably, and give back to their community.

Does this about sum up what you want to achieve?

It may take a few reads of this book to let all the lessons soak in, to improve your money behaviors, and to be in complete flow and rhythm with your numbers. But for now, let's take a look back through the training you have received to arrive at this place. You started by accepting the invitation to dance and being open to learning how to take control of your financials so you can ultimately grow a profitable business (Step 1). You have looked to your past to unearth the source of money beliefs and behaviors that don't serve you. And hopefully you have done the work to heal and resolve childhood memories that have blocked you from dancing with your numbers (Step 2). Or maybe, you have experienced an intervention—a trigger moment—that has encouraged you to make the shift toward a healthier relationship with your numbers (Step 3). Whether it was a desire to be debt free, a drive to achieve a certain profit goal, or an economic recession, these events are opportunities to reframe old unhealthy money scripts and form new ones with the help of financial workshops, resources like these, and financial dance partners.

I have provided the tools and information to strengthen your financial core (Step 4). It takes a while to get to a six pack, but if you followed the guidance in those chapters, your financial operations will be stronger and you will be able to move quicker with reliable information at your fingertips. Weak financial data skews decisions and clouds actions. You can only make the right decisions for your business with accurate, reliable data. In order to be at peak performance, any professional athlete or dancer needs a coach and partner to give tough love and whip them into shape.

Having a strong financial team (Step 5) at each business stage will lead to a financially healthy and stable company with minimal risk of injury due to human error, fraud, or theft. Small businesses without the right financial controls, systems and expertise in place are often limited in their upside potential. Driving sales and converting your goods and services into money is important. But if you don't know how to properly price your offerings to maximize profit and then allocate income received in such a way that you don't run out of cash, it's a wrap for the business. Party done! Hang up your ballet slippers, and take a bow.

Getting to peak financial performance (Step 6) requires more work, discipline, and nuance than just strengthening your core. Your financial dance partners can help you along, but this phase requires continuous internal improvement, which means you're leveraging the numbers to improve every aspect of your business. If sales metrics reflect that you have low win rates, then adjust your sales strategies until you're converting more leads into paying clients. If your capacity utilization is high and employees are overworked, find ways to streamline their workload or hire more people. If client feedback and Google reviews are poor, then work on customer success and culture. And, if you want to pay yourself a higher salary, then do what is needed to increase profit margins. Remember pricing is a lever to drive profits. Considering exiting the business? Then all parts of your corporate body need to be fine-tuned to command an audience of buyers.

At the beginning of this book, I told you I would direct you through a six-part lesson toward *Dancing with Your Numbers*, but I have a surprise and a gift for you. There is a seventh step!

Seven is a perfect number. That's why I saved this one until the end to make sure that you truly take your time doing the work in the prior six lessons to get to this moment because each lesson is meant to build on each other. After being in business for years, you know what you want, what you have time for, and the personal commitment needed to drive this business forward. So the seventh step to dancing with your numbers is to invite others in your community to do the same thing you just did.

Gift your book or purchase a book for another established business owner, especially one humble enough to ask for help and actively seeking guidance from an outsourced CFO, financial consultant, and financial empowerment community. My hope is that millions of you will pass this message along and build a global community of business owners who are rocking their numbers and leveling up to six, seven, eight, or more figures, particularly my fellow women business owners. Let's increase the percent tenfold of woman business owners globally with million-dollar businesses. It is totally possible.

When I asked some of the owners interviewed in this book how they dance with their numbers, they said:

Danielle: "It first started by divorcing myself from my numbers, meaning I used to think they were me. I used to measure my self-worth by how big my numbers were. Dancing with my numbers looks like understanding the relationship with them and my dream life. And knowing that they will help me create that. I used to dance with my numbers like a waltz, a Newtonian dance. Step A comes first, then step B, then step C and we can predict it and it's a linear dance.

Now my dance with the numbers is weightless; it's in space in the galaxy. It's like quantum dance where all past, present, and future versions of me are dancing together with the numbers now."

Ramon: "Find a dance partner. You cannot dance by yourself. I got a dance partner. And that's why, by God's grace I'm debt free cash flow positive, and on the way to wealth building."

Arijit: "In social dance, you have to be ready to make a change and shift your dance moves if someone bumps into you. Likewise, part of being a CEO is being able to react to change when something doesn't go according to plan."

Jennie: "I was not on the same dance floor. I was not even at the party. Before, I didn't even know there was a party. I didn't get the invite. That was before. And now, I'm the host. I love sending out the invitations, and I'm playing the music."

Michael B: "I got into a rhythm, and it was a nice place to be where I was not constantly being stressed by numbers. I wasn't in a place where I was afraid of them anymore and I was able to approach them, talk about the books a little bit, and even get creative with them, which was fun."

Joe: "The way that I dance with my numbers is by not being afraid of the numbers. Tony Robbins talks about dancing with your fear. Instead of allowing fear to control you; instead of allowing the numbers to control you, you control the numbers. You dance with the fear. You lead the dance. I invest in the things that are really important. I used to believe that luxuries are some things that I was not allowed to have. And now I realize that I am manifesting money. I am creating money by being with money and by having a good relationship with money. Now I invest in myself, in a way that I've never given myself permission to do. So the way that I dance with numbers is to make sure that I know my numbers, make sure that I spend time reviewing my numbers, making sure that I spend time with the people in my life who matter and invest in myself."

Luam: "It's a partnership. Sometimes I lead and sometimes my money leads and figure out who is in charge at every moment. It's better when there is a balance. When money leads my life, I need it the most; I'm in a deficit. When I'm leading is when I don't need it. I'm super comfortable, but at those times, maybe I'm not taking enough risk. I'm a dreamer and a visionary and that can lead to risky choices. But I'm also really pragmatic. Really, it's a dance between those two sounds—the pragmatic money holder and the visionary money holder. One is dressed in a business suit, and the other is dressed like Lady Gaga."

Money is a tool to buy back time and freedom. When you use it to invest in your financial education, operations, and advisory team, you will dance with your numbers with the same elation and joy you have when your favorite song comes on the radio. If you want to continue feeling the vibes and working on the core of your business, I'm offering you an opportunity to move beyond this book and put it into practice by shimmying over to the FinCore Studio (https://fincorestrong. com/fincore-studio/). Let's dance with numbers together!

Cheers,
Your chief financial choreographer, *Tricia*

Acknowledgments

To my fellow business owners, if you read all the way through this book to the end and have landed on this page, you deserve to be applauded! I hope that you feel more enlightened, empowered, and engaged with your numbers than ever before. It's been quite a journey writing this book but what kept me steady was YOU! and a deep commitment to use my gifts and knowledge to elevate the financial status and wealth of small business owners, the backbone of the US economy, especially my women and women of color owners.

To my mother, Betty, grandmother, Mary, aunts and all the other women in my family who taught and continue to teach me what good financial stewardship and independence look like, thank you! This book and my life's work is given by God but, fueled by you all.

To my father, John and godfather, Michael for inspiring my love and respect for numbers, thank you!

To my friends, business colleagues, mentors and dance sisters who encouraged my writing process, edited my words, and continue to cheer for every audacious goal and endeavor I undertake, thank you!

Tanya, my Gemini sister, I am so grateful to you for calling me and saying "Don't think about it. Just do it. You've been wanting to write a book for years, just do it already!" I would not be an author today if not for your push. You are one tough cookie, business consultant and life manifester; I appreciate you.

Cynthia Tucker, Eric Koester, Brian Bies, Amanda Brown and the amazing team at the Creator Institute and New Degree Press, thank you for making my dream come true. This experience has been like no other and your guidance every single step of the way has been invaluable. Any first-time author would be lucky to have an all-star team like this!

Caryn Gates, Charles Herold, Geri Stengel, Laurel Carpenter, KC Copeland, my beta readers, thank you!

Raj Bandyopadhyay, my photographer, I appreciate you for capturing the essence of people. Thank you

This book would not have come to life without the honesty, vulnerability and resilience of my interviewees, small business owners who are fluidly dancing with their numbers. To the CEOs listed next and those that remain anonymous, thank you for sharing your expertise and stories.

Arijit Sengupta, CEO Aible.com	Luam Keflezgy, CEO LuamWorld
Danielle Leslie, CEO Culture Add Companies	Malika Jacobs, CEO Kingmakers
Geri Stengel, President Ventureneer	Michael Petrina, CEO Prime Performance & Development
Jennifer Dundas, CEO Blue Marble Ice Cream	Ramon Ray, Editor Zoneofgenius.com
Joe Apfelbaum, CEO AjaxUnion	Rick Kahler, President Kahler Financial Group Inc.
Libby Rothschild, CEO Dietitian Boss	Vivian Chen, CEO Rise

Finally, I want to thank the very generous group of individuals that purchased a copy of this book during the pre-sale. You are the ones that made this publication possible. Thank you for making an investment in me and my writing.

Aimee Wodobode	John Taitt	Niisha Butler
Akshay Shrimanker	John Bonhomme	Nijel Redrick
Al-Nesha Jones	John Smolen	Nikhil Dhongade
Angela Gittens	Jolan Simpson	Patrick Jenkins
Ann Downey	Julbert Abraham	Paul Williams
Arlene Modeste-Knowles	Julia Clark	Peniel Ortega
Ashley Havecker	Julie Cottineau	Quincy Evans
Becky Rogoff	Kathryn Flannery	Raj Bandyopadhyay
Brian Peterson	Keirston R Woods	Ramon Ray
Bryan Block	Kerry Sano	Rev Dr. Sherrylyn Womble
Carlita Ector	Kim Barnes	Romy Parzick
Carolyn Katz	Kinita Copeland	Rose Block
Celli Pitt	Krishanda Leon	Sallie Mullins-Thompon

Chenoa Brown-Pierre	LaNysha Adams, Ph.D	Samantha Pitre Quillen
Chiquita Payne	Laura Kitchings	Sarah Elliott
Christopher Thompson	Leonor Reina	scott fein
Crystal Hardie Langston	Lina Stillman	Shantelle Gammon
Daina Troy	Linh Tran	Sharon Richter
Dawn McGee	Lisa Kuntz	Sherita Gaskins-Tillett
Delfina Warrick	Mareisha Winters	Shernette Palmer
Denica Abdur-Razzaaq	Margaret Wiley	Sheryl Brannon
Denise Simon	Marlon Mathews	Sofia Pertuz
Dionne Gumbs	Mary Meadows Livingston	Sonya Crosswell-Assan
Ean Price Murphy	Mary-Frances Winters	Sophie Wade
Edmund Claude-Williams	Meagan Benz	Stephanie Loayza
Emyliane Christodoulou	Meg Siegal	Suneet Bhatt
Eric Koester	Megan Larson	Tamala Baldwin
Ferrin Coleman	Melissa Gonzales	Tana Kramer
Gabrielle Gayagoy	Melissa Henry	Tanya Alvarez
Gary Ireland	Michael Schreck	Tanya Frias
Georgie-Ann Getton	Michael Bradley	Tara Robinson
Geri Stengel	Michael Ram	Tatianna Mott
Glenn Greenidge	Michelle Awuku-Tatum	Ted Taitt
Harris Tay	Mimi Woods	Thomas Buzzard
Janessa Pulliam	Nancy Martinez	Tulani Thomas
Jeanette Mallory	Nelson Couto	Valerie West
Jenn Feliberty	Nicole Malcolm-Manyara	Yansi Fugel
Jennifer Savino	Nicole McCullum	Zachary Auslander

Appendix

INTRODUCTION

Y, Dr. "Adinkra Symbols and the Rich Akan Culture." *Afrolegends*
(blog). August 27, 2014. https://afrolegends.com/2014/08/27/
adinkra-symbols-and-the-rich-akan-culture/.

CHAPTER 1

DeMers, Jayson. "How Entrepreneurs Get Comfortable with
Being Uncomfortable." *Medium*, November 9, 2020. https://
jaysondemers.medium.com/how-entrepreneurs-get-comfort-
able-with-being-uncomfortable-3507e196a172.

Hayton, James, and Gabriella Cacciotti. "How Fear Helps (and
Hurts) Entrepreneurs." *Harvard Business Review*, April 3, 2018.
https://hbr.org/2018/04/how-fear-helps-and-hurts-entrepre-
neurs.

Northwestern Medicine. "5 Thing You Never Knew About Fear."
Healthbeat (blog), October 2020. https://www.nm.org/health-

beat/healthy-tips/emotional-health/5-things-you-never-knew-about-fear.

CHAPTER 2

Financial Therapy Association. "Home—Financial Therapy Association." 2022. https://financialtherapyassociation.org/.

Marlow, S., and M. McAdam. "Gender and Entrepreneurship: Advancing Debate and Challenging Myths; Exploring the Mystery of the Under-Performing Female Entrepreneur." *International Journal of Entrepreneurial Behavior & Research*, Vol. 19, No. 1 (January 2013): 114-124. https://doi.org/10.1108/13552551311299288.

US Department of Commerce. *Women-Owned Businesses in the 21st Century*. Washington, DC, October 2010. https://www.commerce.gov/sites/default/files/migrated/reports/women-owned-businesses.pdf.

Ventureneer. *The 2018 State of Women Owned Businesses Report*. American Express, 2018. https://ventureneer.com/wp-content/uploads/2018/08/2018-state-of-women-owned-businesses-report_FINAL.pdf.

Visa. "State of Female Entrepreneurship." *She's Next by VISA*, 2019. https://usa.visa.com/content/dam/VCOM/regional/na/us/run-your-business/documents/visa-state-of-entrepreneurship-research-summary.pdf.

CHAPTER 3

Goldman Sachs. "New Survey Data: Amid Rising Delta Variant, Small Businesses Ring the Alarm on Pandemic Recovery," 10,000 Small Businesses, September 14, 2021. https://www.goldmansachs.com/citizenship/10000-small-businesses/US/news-and-program-information/pages/14-sep-2021-survey-release.html .

Prochaska, James O., and Wayne F. Velicer. "The Transtheoretical Model of Health Behavior Change." *American Journal of Health Promotion*, Inc., Vol. 12, No. 1 (Sep-Oct 1997): 38–48. https://web.archive.org/web/20100602085105/http://www.uri.edu/research/cprc/Publications/PDFs/ByTitle/The%20Transtheoretical%20model%20of%20Health%20behavior%20change.pdf.

Wood, Wendy and David T. Neal. "Healthy Through Habit: Interventions for Initiating & Maintaining Health Behavior Change." *Behavioral Science & Policy*, Vol. 2, No. 1 (2016): 71-83.

CHAPTER 4

CB Information Services Inc. "The Top 12 Reasons Startups Fail." *Research Briefs,* August 3, 2021. https://www.cbinsights.com/research/startup-failure-reasons-top/.

US Small Business Administration Office of Advocacy. *Frequently Asked Questions.* Washington, DC: September 2019. https://cdn.advocacy.sba.gov/wp-content/uploads/2019/09/23172241/Frequently-Asked-Questions-Small-Business-20191.pdf.

Chapter 5

Wickman, Gino. *Traction: Get a Grip on Your Business*. Dallas: BenBella Books, Inc., 2011.

CHAPTER 5

DeNicola, Louis. "What is Business Credit, and How Can I Build It?" *Credit Karma*, June 1, 2022. https://www.creditkarma.com/advice/i/build-manage-small-business-credit.

CHAPTER 6

Almquist, Eric, Nicolas Bloch, and John Senior. "The Elements of Value." *Harvard Business Review*, September 2016. https://hbr.org/2016/09/the-elements-of-value

Deloitte Development LLC. "Ten Types of Innovation; the Discipline of Building Breakthroughs." *Doblin*, 2022. https://doblin.com/ten-types.

Griffith, Erin. "Why Startups Fail, According to Their Founders." *Fortune*, September 25, 2014. https://fortune.com/2014/09/25/why-startups-fail-according-to-their-founders/.

Hunter, G. Shawn. "Out Think: How Innovative Leaders Drive Exceptional Outcomes." Canada: John Wiley & Sons Canada, Ltd., 2013. Quoted in Peek, Sean. "Creativity Is Not Innovation (But You Need Both)." *Business News Daily*, July 23, 2021. https://www.businessnewsdaily.com/6848-creativity-vs-innovation.html.

Wickman, Gino. *Traction: Get a Grip on Your Business*. Dallas: BenBella Books, Inc., 2011.

CHAPTER 7

Bailey, Dave. "How to Build Relationships with Investors Before You Need Their Money." *Inc*, April 3, 2017. https://www.inc.com/dave-bailey/how-to-build-relationships-with-investors-before-you-need-their-money.html.

Churchill, Neil C., and Virginia L. Lewis. "The Five Stages of Small Business Growth." *Harvard Business Review*, May 1983. https://hbr.org/1983/05/the-five-stages-of-small-business-growth.

Hendricks, Gay. *The Big Leap: Conquer Your Hidden Fear and Take Life to the Next Level*. New York: Harper Collins Publishers, 2010.

CHAPTER 8

Elrod, Hal. *The Miracle Morning: The Not-So-Obvious Secret Guaranteed to Transform Your Life (Before 8AM)*. Hal Elrod International, Inc., 2012.

US Small Business Administration. "Close or Sell Your Business." *Business Guide*. Accessed July 5, 2022. https://www.sba.gov/business-guide/manage-your-business/close-or-sell-your-business.